A History of
FLOWER
ARRANGEMENT

Lots of love on Mother's day
and lots of love for the
rest of the year,

Christine x.

1984

Frontispiece: "A Bouquet of Flowers," by the Flemish painter Nicholas van Veerendael (1640-1691).

A HISTORY OF
FLOWER
ARRANGEMENT

Revised Edition

JULIA S. BERRALL

THAMES AND HUDSON

ACKNOWLEDGMENTS

One cannot assemble the material for a book such as this without at some time seeking the advice and knowledge of specialists in the field of decorative arts and horticulture. I am immeasurably grateful to the museum staff members and to the librarians of special collections who took an interest in my project and shared with me their knowledge, in several instances guiding me to unknown source materials. Mr. Na-sun Wu's deep and scholarly understanding of Chinese art was an inspiration in writing about the flowers of his country, and Mr. Jiro Harada of the Tokyo National Museum gave invaluable help in providing photographs of flower arrangements from his native country. Private collectors who have graciously allowed me to use their books or reproduce their paintings and engravings include Mrs. Bartlett Arkell; Mr. Henderson Inches; Mrs. Roy Arthur Hunt; Sir Alec Martin; Mr. Edward G. Robinson; Mrs. John Slade; and Mrs. Roy Tomlinson. To Dr. Harold Moldenke and Mr. Ben Blackburn I extend my thanks for horticultural information generously provided, and to my cousin Gertrude Smith Wister, an ever present and never failing source of horticultural knowledge, I owe an especial debt of gratitude.

JULIA S. BERRALL

First published in Great Britain in 1953 by
Thames and Hudson Ltd, London
This revised and enlarged edition published in 1969
Reprinted 1978

Printed in Great Britain by William Clowes & Sons Limited
London, Beccles and Colchester

CONTENTS

INTRODUCTION

FLOWER ARRANGEMENT is an art. Its recognition and popularity and the interest and enthusiasm brought to it in America during the past forty years have undoubtedly been heightened by the garden-club movement, which provides the competition and stimulation of local and national flower shows.

The fundamental reasons, however, for its well-nigh universal appeal stem from the fact that it is a practical visual art happily adapted to satisfy the need of the averge person for creative self-expression. Flowers and foliage are readily available from garden, field, or flower shop, and it is not difficult to assemble a few suitable vases, holders, and sharp cutting tools. In fact, expenses are just exactly what one makes them. Ingenuity, a sense of color, and a basic understanding of design are the deciding factors in creating a really successful arrangement. These are the same talents called into play in any form of interior decorating.

When the practice of an art grows rapidly, as this has done in our country, a time inevitably comes when we should stop and evaluate the situation. It is the easiest thing in the world to grow hidebound by technicalities and a too literal-minded conception of "rules." A study of the past not only throws some light on the development of present-day styles, but at times provides refreshingly different points of view, as well as new inspiration, for the homemaker who wishes to decorate her period rooms with suitably combined flowers and vases. Furthermore, the exhibitor at a flower show, competing in classes which are planned to evoke certain historical periods, is naturally interested in all it is possible to learn about past fashions in flower arrangement and the actual flowers that were used.

With this in mind, the author has devoted herself to exhaustive research both here and abroad. It is amazing how little written or illustrative material exists which might enable us to say, for instance, that "in the Georgian period in England flowers were arranged thus and so," or that "the Chinese have always placed flowers in vases in this manner." As we shall see, certain periods and countries give us much more material than others.

A key fact that emerges clearly, however, is that there have been two main trends in the art of arranging flowers, and these have been our sources of inspiration. One stems from the Orient, the other from Europe.

The art of flower arrangement has been practiced in Japan for well over a thousand years, although it was not a home art (as opposed to a temple art) until the fifteenth century. It reached its height in the eighteenth century, by which time a number of rules had been formalized and much symbolism had become associated with the entire art. Strictly speaking, classic Japanese flower art depends on an asymmetrical, purely linear design, based on three main lines of related height proportions. This dynamic and rhythmic art lays a great deal more stress on silhouette, or line, than it does on color.

It was the Chinese who first contributed to the development of the art of flower arranging. Contemplative, and with a characteristically sensitive appreciation of nature, the Chinese learned to enjoy the quiet beauty of a few perfect blossoms or a branch of interesting shape. This refined taste was passed on to Japan, along with Buddhism, and developed into their highly symbolic art. The Chinese way of arranging flowers has never been as obviously studied or stylized as that of the Japanese. However subtle the differences may be between the two, we recognize that we are indebted to both these peoples for their appreciation of line in flower design, as well as for their emphasis on the individual form, texture, and color of a few chosen blooms.

In direct contrast, Europeans have always been inclined to gather mixed bouquets. Religion and philosophy have had little, if anything, to do with their handling of flowers. Their use of floral colors and forms has much diversity, and of course includes a quantity of bulbous material not grown in the Orient. The selection of gay colors, arranged in mass, has undoubtedly been due to the more exuberant and outgoing character of the Occidental, including both English and Americans. By present-day standards, however, this type of flower ornamentation should be considered strictly as assembled bouquets, rather than as flower arrangement in the true sense of the word. However, the Dutch and Flemish flower painters of the seventeenth and eighteenth centuries, as well as the French painters and engravers of the same period, while intensely interested in horticulture, composed their canvases with such skill that they have much to teach us today about handling a quantity of flowers in a large arrangement.

The great interest in horticulture exemplified by the seventeenth century painters continued for the next two hundred years. Both in England and in America, the eighteenth century was a time of much plant exploration, plant classification, and plant propagation. The natural result in the nineteenth century was that gardening was practiced to some extent by everyone who owned a plot of ground, and the average housewife picked a sampling of her garden and brought the bouquet indoors to brighten the dining table or the living room.

The love of flowers has not abated. With increased leisure, due to the trend toward smaller homes and labor-saving devices, women have gradually found additional time to devote to favorite occupations and to develop many incidental duties into an art.

When the garden-club movement really got into full swing in our country in the 1920's, members began looking for rules whereby flowers could be arranged to the best advantage. As a result of considerable observation on the part of garden enthusiasts who traveled around the world and saw how flowers were utilized for decoration in other countries, certain rules became accepted. The first and best-known of these, that a flower arrangement should be at least one and a half times the height of the container, is taken verbatim from the Japanese. Other principles stemming from Japan were subsequently adopted.

As our experience in this new visual art widened and its popularity gained ground, we found that many of the time-tried art principles used by the painter could help us in achieving other desirable effects. Seventeenth century Dutch and Flemish flower pieces, which often included still-life objects, taught us much about the massing of color as well as about composition; from them, little secrets of placement were learned in giving flower arrangements third dimension, or depth. Though we were working in a three-dimensional medium, we still had lessons to learn from the two-dimensional canvases of the masters.

It was natural that the influences of Europe and Asia should meet in America as public and private collections of paintings from all over the world grew in importance. These collections, of course, included floral subjects. At the same time, countless books on flowers and their arrangement were published or imported. Professional horticulturalists, decorators, and flower arrangers came to these shores from the continent of Europe, from England, and from Japan. They gave lectures and demonstrations, and frequently opened businesses and stayed on. Each has had an influence on the trend in America today, but no one group of persons, nor any country, can be said to be responsible for our present taste in flower arrangement as now displayed at flower-show exhibitions and in our homes.

The art of flower arrangement in America has its own individuality. Though we probably owe more to Japan than to any other single country, especially in certain formulated rules, in the final analysis our flower arrangements are quite different from theirs. We combine attention to both line and mass, we use color more freely than they, and we express ourselves without oriental restraint. On the other hand, our effects are often more studied than those in European flower arrangement, for we have made more use of line, and even in our predominantly mass arrangements our results are less bouquet-like.

In the preparation of this book, I have gone directly to the available source-material on the art of flower arrangement, and have conscientiously studied all possible clues. One conclusion I have reached is that the phrase *period styles of arranging* is not applicable to all our study, for only in Japan, in the United States, and to some extent in Great Britain during the last hundred years do we find any system of rules for the assembly of plant-material. We must realize that the floral art of Europe has generally tended to be a *bouquet art*, without any rigid school of thought, while that of the Far East has been a *linear, or restrained art*, based on philosophic and religious principles.

The purpose of this book has been to gather and to interpret in one volume as much source-material as possible from various periods and countries. I have purposely confined the illustrations and discussions to showing the use of cut flowers in vases, feeling that a consideration of general floral decoration might rather confuse than clarify our principles. Natural and realistic representations which are practical to study have been stressed. On the other hand, the highly conventionalized and decorative styles of the artist-designer have been omitted, since these have little bearing on the subject of the use of flowers in the home. Charming as they may be as paintings or decorations, the stylized flower and vase motifs of Persia have not been included, nor have certain peasant arts such as Pennsylvania German. No general book could include all the best examples of such prolific schools as the Dutch or Flemish; yet everything of special interest that could be found in certain other significant periods, such as the early English, appears here.

The illustrative material has been gathered from many sources and consists mainly of reproductions of paintings, engravings, tapestries, and illuminated manuscripts. These represent the only valid record of earlier days, before the camera was known. In some of these illustrations, the grouping of flowers in a vase may have been incidental to a portrayal of the daily life and accepted social customs of our forebears. Such composite studies are particularly interesting to us, for the costumes of the people or the decorative style of a room frequently place the general period of the flower arrangement more quickly than the mere reading of a date could do, and this association is more readily retained in the memory.

It is particularly recommended that the flower arranger should, in studying the illustrations in this book, look for the visual answers to a group of five key questions which I list here for his or her convenience.

1. In what kinds of vases have the flowers been placed?

2. Where, within the home, have flowers been used?

3. What are the typical kinds of flowering material of each historical period and country discussed, and do we see the introduction of new or unusual flowers as the story progresses?

4. Can we detect a characteristic style of arranging among the different groupings of the same period?

5. In what ways can examples of beautiful flower groupings of the past be of use in contemporary adaptations?

IN THE TIME OF THE ANCIENTS

FLORAL DECORATION may be said to be as old as civilization itself. Ever since the early days of recorded history, when man was at last able to free himself from the necessities of the hunt and till the soil for his living instead, floral decoration has played an important part in his arts.

The remains of many ancient cultures provide us with ample proof that people have always been appreciative of the beauties of nature; they show that flowers have been a never-failing source of inspiration for the adornment of architecture, utensils, and other objects of daily use. On occasion we get glimpses of a more intimate use of flowers and see vases of cut blossoms decorating the home or presented as offerings. Sometimes the record is full and clear, at other times the mists of antiquity make the search difficult and tenuous. Yet there are always clues to tell us that people in the past brought flowers indoors to be enjoyed just as we today fill vases with flowers to beautify our rooms.

Ample evidence exists to show that the ancient Egyptians decorated with cut flowers placed in vases. Many wall paintings and bas-reliefs in Egyptian tombs tell us what flower vases looked like in those far-off days, with what they were filled, and when and how they were used.

The art of the ancient Egyptian was highly stylized, and the natural form of the lotus or water-lily[1] readily lent itself to conventionalization. Since the lotus was the flower of the goddess Isis and therefore considered sacred, we encounter it time and time again throughout the whole course of Egyptian art. We can trace it as far back as 2500 B.C. in vases of extraordinary interest (Fig. 1). These were made either of glass or of heavily glazed and decorated blue faience and have extra spout-like openings at the sides. The glass containers were set inside red terra cotta cups which in turn rested on stands. In the Metropolitan Museum there is a blue faience vase, with similar spouts for holding flowers, also decorated with lotus motifs, dating from the 12th dynasty (Fig. 2). It is a small scale-model included with many other objects of considerably less than life-size which were entombed with the departed in order to supply him with the necessities of daily living during his long journey to the next world. These two particular vases seem to set a pattern for functionalism. About four thousand years later the idea recurs in Persia (Fig. 3) and in Holland (Fig. 4). The occurrence of the similar form, in instances so widely separated in both time and space, may be explained by the fact that the heavy-headed tulip, so commonly grown in both these countries, needed support just as the lotus did in ancient Egypt.

We know that bowls of flowers were set on the banquet tables of the Egyptians (Fig. 5), and that precious gold and silver vases filled with lotus blossoms and buds were borne in processions and sometimes offered as tribute. A picture of the workshop of two metal workers shows us several such vases, of beautiful craftsmanship (Fig. 7). They appear to

[1] Horticulturists and archaeologists are now in agreement as to the exact identification of the erroneously named Egyptian "lotus." *Nelumbium speciosum* or *nucifera* (the true lotus) is not indigenous to Egypt, and neither its pink hue nor its distinctive seed vessel has ever appeared in ancient Egyptian art. The blue and white water lilies *(nymphaea)* still abundant in the calm waters of the Nile delta are the flowers the ancients knew. The *nymphaea lotus* is a large, white, night-blooming variety, with flowers five to ten inches across; the *Nymphaea caerulea* (most frequently seen in paintings) is a smaller-flowered, blue variety.

Figure 2. Turquoise pottery model of an Egyptian flower vase. 2400-1800 B.C. Conventionalized lotus decoration.

Figure 1. One of a pair of lotus-filled vases dating from about 2500 B.C., in the painted wall decoration of the tombs of Beni Hasan, Egypt.

Figure 3. XVIIth-century Persian vase of brown pottery.

Figure 4. XVIIth-century Delft flower holder.

Metropolitan Museum of Art

Left: Figure 5. Stone relief from the Old Kingdom tomb of Pernēb, showing a bowl filled with lotus blossoms and buds.

Below: Figure 6. Lotus-filled bowl being carried in a procession. Painted bas-relief from the Middle Kingdom Temple of Se'n-wasret I.

Opposite page: Figure 7. Egyptian artisans at work. This detail from a painted wall decoration in the tomb of the Two Sculptors at Thebes shows three elaborately designed metal vases, one of which holds lotus blossoms. The original pieces probably were decorated with inset fragments of colorful stones or paste. The ornateness of these vases suggests that they were probably intended for ceremonial use or for tribute. XVIIIth dynasty.

have been decorated with inset fragments of stone or paste. Because of their elaborateness, we judge they must have been intended for ceremonial use.

For almost three thousand years, Egyptian art changed very little. This lack of change was possible because rules were formalized and laid down for the artist to follow. During the time of the Pharaohs the lotus, the papyrus plant and the palm tree were the most commonly portrayed members of the plant kingdom.[2] *Carthamus tinctorius* (safflower or false safron), *Malva alcea* (a mallow), and *Papaver rhoeas* (corn poppy) have been found in mortuary garlands. Although the rose was depicted in certain early wall paintings, it was not until the Ptolemaic era (*circa* 323–31 B.C.) that it appeared with any frequency. It is probable that this flower came to Egypt from Greece. With the spread of Greco-Roman culture, many flowers must have been introduced. Our clues in tracing them come from perfume recipes, from the preserved remains of flower garlands found on mummies, and from the writings of Plato,[3] Pliny,[4] and Dioscorides.[5] A list of flowers which have been positively identified includes the following: *Acacia Farnesiana, Acorus Calamus* (sweet flag), *Anemone coronaria* (poppy-flowered anemone), *Celosia argentea cristata* (cockscomb), *Centaurea depressa, Chrysanthemum coronarium* (garland chrysanthemum or crown daisy, annual), *Convolvulus scoparius, Crinum abyssinicum, Delphinium orientale, Erigeron aegyptiacus, Iris sibirica* (Siberian iris), *Jasminum Sambac* (Arabian jasmine), *Lathyrus sativus* (grass pea), *Lawsonia inermis* (henna), *Lupinus Termis* (Egyptian lupine), *Narcissus Tazetta* (Polyanthus Narcissus), *Papaver somniferum* (opium poppy), *Rosa sancta* or *Richardii,* and *Scilla pusilla.*

[2] In the Great Temple of Thutmose III at Karnak dating from about 1450 B.C. there is a stone bas-relief which shows some 275 plants, but these were said to grow in Syria, and Thutmose had them carved as a record of his Syrian campaign.

[3] Plato, the Greek philosopher and writer, (427–347 B.C.), traveled extensively to Egypt, Cyrenaica, Italy, and Sicily.

[4] Pliny the Elder, the Roman author (62–113 A.D.), wrote a *Natural History* which included an herbal combining both Greek and Roman plant knowledge.

[5] Dioscorides was a Greek physician who traveled with the Roman armies during the 1st century A.D. His *De Materia Medica* was a collection of information concerning plants, particularly the medicinal ones, which remained the authoritative work on botany and medicine for fifteen centuries.

13

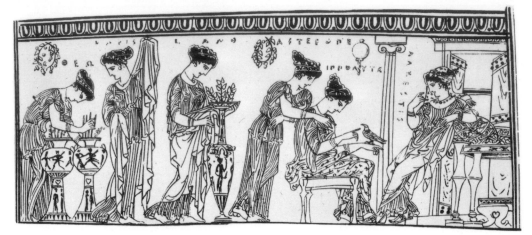

Figure 8. Bridal scene. A very rare Grecian example of decorated terra cotta showing plant materials in vases. The vase shapes depicted are peculiar to weddings and the leafy branches are probably olive. The thigh guard which includes this scene as part of its decoration dates from the late fifth century B.C.

Strangely enough, when our search takes us to ancient Greece and Rome, there is little reward. Greek and Roman writers tell us that flowers played an important and significant role in the daily life of the people, but their use was confined almost entirely to the making of wreaths and garlands, and there is negligible evidence that they were ever cut and placed in vases. Figure 8 shows one of the every few known instances in which what we might call a vase of flowers is even approximated. Yet actually flowers are entirely lacking here, as in all Greek examples. The leafy branches shown in the large vase and being placed in the smaller ones are probably of olive, for this is a bridal scene; the olive was associated, among other things, with weddings.

It seems almost incredible that, of all the thousands of Greek vases, not one was made solely for the purpose of holding flowers. As we study these vases and the interesting figures and scenes which decorate them, and as we examine the statues of both Greece and Rome and the paintings of the latter, it becomes evident that the wearing of wreaths or chaplets on the head and garlands around the neck was quite usual. Indeed, this was where the interest in flowers as decoration was centered. We learn, further, that there were professional makers (Darius is said to have had forty-six of them in his household) and sellers of these ubiquitous wreaths; and there were, of course, gardeners who grew the necessary plants. These included the rose (most popular of all), violet, lily, cornflower, iris, hawthorn, acacia, lychnis, helenium, cyclamen, the saffron crocus, and certain native shrubs. Ivy, laurel, olive, oak, and grape were commonly used, and certain aromatic herbs such as mint, thyme, rosemary and marjoram are also mentioned in the ancient writings. There were many occasions when crowns or garlands were exchanged or given. Athletes, poets, civic leaders, and victorious soldiers and sailors were awarded wreaths; and garlands were exchanged by lovers, worn at weddings, and hung on a door to denote the birth of a son. The custom of wearing wreaths was so widespread it has been suggested that the garland-makers were the flower arrangers of their day.

The use of rose blossoms and petals during the festivities of the decadent years of the declining Roman Empire was lavish and almost fantastic. Roses were strewn on banquet tables and couches, streets and lakes; both Nero and Cleopatra used them extravagantly in all sorts of entertainments and ceremonies. Twelve varieties are known to have been in cultivation, for Pliny mentioned them in his Natural History; the cabbage rose, or *Rosa centifolia,* was one of them. How enough plants were grown to fill the constant demand for flowers is hard to imagine, but it is known that flowers were shipped overseas from Egypt to Rome, and it is said that the Romans eventually managed to force them to bloom out of season by growing them among hot water pipes.

The next step along our path of exploration brings us to a world-famous Roman mosaic, the *Basket of Flowers* (Fig. 9) now in the Vatican Museum. This was found near Tivoli, at Hadrian's villa. It is said to date from the beginning of the second century A.D.,

Figure 9. Roman mosaic, IInd century. The basket holds roses, Roman hyacinths, a double anemone, tulips, red carnations, and a blue morning glory. The basket motif recurs throughout the history of art, from this early period to the Victorian era.

and it shows a grouping of mixed flowers for the first time. There has been some controversy over this particular mosaic, for it includes tulips, which are seen at the right side of the arrangement. Those who remember that the tulip is said to have been known first in central Europe and Holland in the sixteenth century, may doubt the authenticity of the mosaic for this reason, especially since it is known that there was restoration work done on it after its discovery in the eighteenth century. Authorities state, however, that the restorations were made only on the background. That *Tulipa gesneriana,* from Asia, was early known in Italy is supported by the fact that it is clearly identifiable in the decoration of a Milanese manuscript, circa 1100, owned by the Pierpont Morgan Library in New York. In Pena and De l'Obel's herbal, the *Adversaria* (London, 1570), the author says: "I have seen them (tulips) at Venice and Padua, and it has been some years since they came from Greece and Macedonia." In the previous century, Giampietrino also had displayed them prominently in a painting. It would thus seem that Southern Europeans knew the tulip considerably earlier than their neighbors to the north. The flowers in the mosaic basket provide a delightful combination of colors and forms. Roses, tulips, and carnations, as well as the morning glory, the hyacinth, and the double anemone, give us our first glimpse of a truly naturalistic flower bouquet. The colors are mellow, yet still true to life, and include several variations of pink, rose, red, green, pale yellow, blue, and white.

With the decline of Rome, the flower art of the ancients seemed to go into eclipse with all civilization. There was a long pause for the duration of the Dark Ages before the artists and writers of Medieval Europe and the Renaissance recorded the floral customs of their times.

Opposite: Figure 10. "Maiden Gathering Flowers." Wall painting found at Stabiae, a town destroyed by Vesuvius in A.D. 79. The flowers were probably asphodel and recall the lines in Homer's Odyssey:

"And Rest at Last where Souls Unbodied Dwell
In Everlasting Medes of Asphodel."

Figure 11. Leonardo da Vinci included a delicate flower-filled vase in his painting of the Virgin and Child.

MEDIEVAL EUROPE AND THE ITALIAN RENAISSANCE

WITHIN THE SECLUSION of monastery walls, gardening flourished quietly during medieval times. Outside, warring feudal lords kept the countryside in a constant state of unrest, although farming, of necessity, went on. Inside the monasteries, the monks busied themselves growing the herbs and simples for medicine and the fruits and vegetables necessary for their table. Flower gardens as such did not exist. We know, however, that the monks were well acquainted with many of the beautiful everyday flowers, for exquisite glimpses of them appear in the illuminated manuscripts over which they toiled so faithfully.

Art belonged primarily to the Church during this period. Stained-glass windows, mosaics, tapestries, sculpture, paintings, and illuminated religious books all served to illustrate the Christian faith, express its aspiration, and embellish its observance. Upon occasion we get glimpses of secular life, for of course the lords in the castles hired artists to decorate for them also. By the beginning of the fifteenth century, perhaps with a lessening of absolute faith and certainly with a demand for more naturalism in art, painters sometimes used, as backgrounds for their religious paintings, such natural-looking and homelike scenes that they spring to life even now. In the Annunciation scene (Fig. 11) painted by The Master of Flémalle, we see, surrounded by the most casual of everyday objects, the Virgin receiving the heavenly messenger. The symbolical Annunciation lilies have been placed on the table in an ordinary pottery jug, and if common field flowers had been placed there instead, we should feel that we had been invited right into a typical fifteenth-century home.

The little manuscript illumination (Fig. 13) also serves to point out that flowers have not always been placed in containers which were made especially to hold them. Ordinary objects of everyday use have always been pressed into service whenever needed to hold the simple bouquets gathered with so much affection. Humble glass tumblers, earthenware jugs, or the majolica drug jars known as *albarelli* have all been used, as well as regular vases; and one frequently sees specifically ecclesiastical containers in the religious paintings (Fig. 14).

In looking at all the beautiful Annunciation scenes, we may rejoice at finding so many examples of flowers grouped in vases, but we must remember there is more than mere decoration connected with their presence. There is always symbolism of a high order in the flowers we see represented, and this in itself is a subject for study. Up until the sixteenth century, flowers were introduced in painting to express certain abstract concepts such as love, purity, and humility. The rose, which Sappho had called the Queen of Flowers, soon became the emblem of The Queen of Heaven to the early Christian mystics. In ancient times it had been the flower of Venus, goddess of love, and with the revival of interest in classical subjects during the Renaissance it once again appeared as her attribute. Therefore we see the rose portrayed in subjects representing either sacred or profane love. The white *Lilium candidum,* cultivated in Europe since earliest times, had become the symbol of fertility and chastity. Nothing could possibly have been more appropriate to symbolize the miraculous birth, and the flower appeared in so many paintings of the Annunciation that it soon was called the Madonna Lily. Before this lily was introduced in Northern Europe, Flemish artists used the iris for the Virgin's flower, and in all Roman

Brussels National Museum

Left: Figure 12. "The Annunciation," painted by the Master of Flémalle. The naturalness of the entire setting suggests that flowers in vases were commonplace touches even in the early fifteenth century.

Opposite page: Figure 15. Detail from the central panel of the Portinari Altarpiece painted by Hugo Van der Goes, around 1475. The everyday character of the flower containers—a majolica drug jar and a glass tumbler—are of interest, as is the symbolical selection of the flowers themselves. The seven fully-opened columbine flowers represent the seven gifts of the Holy Spirit: wisdom, understanding, counsel, strength, knowledge, true godliness, and holy fear. They are placed in glass, which denotes purity. The iris and the lily (in this instance, Lilium bulbiferum) are dedicated to the Virgin.

Right: Figure 13. Illuminated "Book of Hours," Flemish, early XVIth century. Even though there is symbolism in the selection of flowers, the little jug, the glass tumbler, and the two-handled bottle in which the flowers are placed suggest the casual and natural gesture of bringing cut flowers indoors.

Extreme right: Figure 14. An ecclesiastical container, a metal ewer, is shown in this detail of an altarpiece by the master of the Saint Barbara Legend. XVth century.

Walters Art Gallery, Baltimore

Metropolitan Museum of Art

Uffizi Gallery, Florence

21

C. von Pannwitz Collection

Figure 16. The Flemish painter, Gerard David (c. 1460-1523) has painted here one of the most charming of all Madonnas. The great appeal of the painting lies in the informality and everyday character of the scene, which shows the Babe being fed his broth beside a table on which is placed a vase holding simple garden flowers: iris, rocket, columbine, roses, and heartsease.

Opposite page: Figure 17. "The Annunciation," by the XVth-century Umbrian painter known as the Master of the Barberini Panels. Pink and white roses are shown in a classic Renaissance vase. The Virgin receives the angel in the loggia which connects house and garden.

Catholic countries the snowdrop was also dedicated to the Virgin Mary. The pink *(Dianthus)* represented divine love when shown with Her, but if it was held in the hand of a sitter for a secular painting, it often denoted a betrothal.

The seven-fold gifts of the Holy Ghost were represented by doves and also by the columbine (the name of which comes from the Latin word *columbinus,* meaning dovelike). Artists carefully placed seven blooms in their pictures to carry out the idea; these can easily be counted in the Portinari Altarpiece flowers (Fig. 15). Among other symbols, the violet typified humility. The clover because of its leaf and the pansy or heartsease (*viola tricolor*) because of its three-colored petals both represented the Trinity; and the lily-of-the-valley quite naturally was another flower signifying purity. Both the fruit and the flower of the strawberry are often seen represented, particularly in the old manuscripts. They were thought to symbolize the fruits of the spirit, or the rewards that were bestowed on the righteous believer for his good deeds.

Along with the revival of learning during the Renaissance, people began to take an interest in gardening. As part of the great revolution that took place with the invention of printing, the woodcut and movable type soon made the herbal a reasonably accessible book, and printed editions of the classic works on botany of Pliny, Theophrastus,[1] and Dioscorides, hitherto only available in manuscript form, were published.

The Italians became justly famous for their extensive gardens, and flowers were grown for the sake of their beauty instead of for the utilitarian purposes which had been taught in the herbals. The fourteenth-century garden was still essentially like the Medieval walled garden. Its rectangular beds were divided between herbs, such as mint, rosemary, thyme, basil, sage, and rue, also flowers, such as roses, violets, irises, lilies, and more exotic flowers which had been brought in by trade from the East and which included jasmine, hyacinths, and lilacs. A large variety of fruit trees was cultivated, and roses were often planted for hedges or grown over trellises. The double pink or white *Rosa alba* and the

[1] Theophrastus, a Greek botanist (372–287 B.C.), wrote a *History of Plants* and a treatise called *Theoretical Botany.*

23

Above: Figure 18. Detail from the painting "Madonna and Child," by Botticini (1477-1520). Saint John is shown holding a glass vase, very possibly Venetian, in which there is a tight little bunch of roses.

Right: Figure 19. "Virgin and Child with Saint John," by Botticelli (1446-1510). Piled high with the pink and white roses (Rosa alba) of the Renaissance, these beautiful flower holders suggest altar decorations.

Extreme left: Figure 20. Late Renaissance metal vase of Florentine make. A similar one is to be seen in the portrait of a Medici lady by Sustermans.

Left: Figure 21. Detail from the painting "A Lady of the Medici Court," by Justus Sustermans (1597-1681).

red *Rosa gallica* were the Renaissance roses. The cabbage rose or *Rosa centifolia* was lost to Italy at the time but was re-introduced later from Holland.

One of the most charming features of the Italian garden was the lawn of fine grass in which various kinds of small flowers were allowed to grow. Instead of remaining two separate entities, soon the house and garden were brought into closer relationship by the loggia, and the symmetry of the flower beds suggested the introduction of further architectural forms. Thus, within a space of a hundred years, the entire conception of the garden changed. Terraces and steps, statues and fountains, pavilions and pergolas, marble seats and flower vases, further set off by topiary work and columnar cypresses, all made a completely formal setting.

In the late sixteenth century, we find that flower beds were relegated to small spaces near the houses, in what were called "secret" gardens. Perhaps it was in such a spot that the flowers to fill the vase shown in Figure 22 were gathered. This bouquet includes a number of flowers we are to see time and time again during the sixteenth, seventeenth, and eighteenth centuries. Narcissus, tulips, hyacinths, anemones, both single and double, and carnations make an impressive showing in this ingenious covered urn. Ingenuity goes one step further in another perforated urn which was designed to be completely leak-proof (Fig. 23). These engravings come from an interesting Italian garden book published in Rome in 1633, written by P. Giovanni Battista Ferrari of Sienna, and entitled *Flora —ouero Cultura di Fiori*. The book contains chapters on the culture of certain popular flowers, together with hints on good gardening and various methods of decorating with flowers. These are astonishing in their virtuosity, and many of the suggestions for the care of cut flowers are exactly those which we follow today. A custom of decorating baskets of varying shapes with flowers is described which sounds most elaborate, for it includes the actual weaving of the basket itself of pliable willow twigs called osiers. Flowers were apparently inserted in the woven sides of the basket, and a grounding of myrtle was done first. The whole basket was meant to be covered with flowers, and it was strongly advised that they often be sprayed with water. These floral decorations, probably similar to the one shown in the earlier Flemish engraving symbolizing Smell (Fig. 26), are spoken of as "gracious offerings" to Princes or, as in one case which is mentioned in the book, to a Cardinal. Apparently they played an important part in the pageantry of the High Renaissance and the Baroque period which followed. The author describes one such decoration made in the shape of a sailing ship, but he notes that this particular fashion died out, as it was "so much work."

In this same book careful thought is also given the assembling of bouquets, to carry or to give away; the author shows how they were tied together, with all flower heads turning out, the most important flower at the center top, and the stems neatly covered by narcissus leaves laid over them lengthwise and tied with thread. Another chapter tells how to preserve and dry flowers in their natural colors by gently burying them in clean, sun-dried sand (this for sterilization) and allowing them to remain in a sun-heated place for several months before uncovering. Victorian writers described a similar method to their readers, and even today it is not unusual to find articles in garden magazines which explain how to preserve flowers in borax or silica gel.

From this truly fascinating book, one would gather that the fashionable way of displaying flowers in the years just following the Italian Renaissance (the period which we now refer to as Baroque) was to insert them in vases so that only the flower heads showed (Fig. 22). In order that the flowers might each be fully viewed and not be crushed by their neighbors, they were poked into their containers through equi-distant holes. Flowers and vase became a rather stiff display, rather than a graceful arrangement. Within a short time the French Baroque style of the seventeenth century was to emphasize sweeping lines and gracefully curving stems, while the painters of the Low Countries treated their flowers in the most natural manner of all.

Pierpont Morgan Library, New York

Left: Figure 22. Illustration from Ferrari's "Flora ouero Cultura di Fiori." Rome, 1638. This pottery vase had a removable lid through which the flower stems were inserted. Directions were given in this old garden book for freshening the flowers by removing the lid—flowers and all—changing the water, and recutting the stems. It was also suggested that the water be changed every three days.

Right: Figure 23. Also from Ferrari's "Flora." The makers of this remarkable vase were Fabritio Sbardoni and Giovani Tattista Martelletti, described as being famous for growing flowers and arranging them artistically. No mention is made of the material of which the vase was made, but it stood four hands high and, when filled with water, was heavy enough to remain steady. A little study will reveal how the entire vase could be filled with water without any leakage from the holes. When the first catch basin at the top was filled, it overflowed into the little pipe leading down to the next layer. This in turn filled up gradually and then overflowed down its pipe, and so on all the way to the bottom. This vase was designed for use with short-stemmed flowers, so that the shape of the vase was preserved. In the shallow shells over the masks small bunches of varied flowers were to be placed "like pearls in an oyster." At the very top the best or most strikingly beautiful flower was to be placed, Ferrari declaring that if it were of a quivering kind it would "jokingly applaud its own triumphant beauty."

26

Above: Figure 24. Early XVIIth-century Italian still life by a follower of Caravaggio. The contrast of the dark vase with the clear glass one is striking. The flowers are gracefully displayed, although the arrangements are really "one-of-a-kind" collections. Roses, pinks, bulbous iris, rosemary, a double anemone, calendula, French marigold, Tazetta narcissus, cornflower, orange blossoms, veronica, jasmine, and small pansies are all included. In the Hermitage in Leningrad, there is a very beautiful painting of a lute player by Caravaggio that includes a glass vase of flowers quite similar in feeling.

Right: Figure 25. Early XVIIth-century still life (detail) by the German artist Georg Flegel. The vase of precious metal holds a colorful assortment of flowers: rose-colored tulips, white narcissus, pinks, a bright red anemone, and a pink rose.

DUTCH AND FLEMISH
FLOWER PAINTINGS

Up TO THE SEVENTEENTH CENTURY, as we have seen, flowers often appeared incidentally in paintings of religious subjects and classical allegories, in portraiture, and in the landscape. The patrons of art had been the Church and the nobility.

Now however, economic conditions had changed radically. We need only recall the discovery, during the previous century, of new worlds across the seas to imagine the great changes of the period. The religious turmoil of the Reformation had already had tremendous impact and new social trends became apparent. The bourgeois man of the middle class now rose to the top position in government and business. He was the new patron and collector of art.

Nowhere was this more apparent than in Holland. The prosperous Dutch traders soon became interested in having themselves and their newly acquired art objects, such as Venetian glass and Turkish rugs, painted for posterity. With the Reformation, the Church had lost its predominant place as the patron of all arts in the Protestant countries. Artists now turned not only to genre painting and portraiture, but, luckily for us, to the flower piece and still-life. Long skilled in the delicate portrayal of flowers, adept at catching surface reflections and the textural qualities of drapery, the Flemish painters as well as the Dutch had all the necessary qualifications for revealing the beauty to be found in the combination of flowers, fruits, and everyday objects. There are hundreds of their flower pieces which we might study with profit, scattered throughout the museums and private collections of the world.

The real story of Western flower arranging should, in truth, begin at this point, for the beautiful and often opulent flower paintings of these seventeenth century Dutch and Flemish masters have served as object lessons in the grouping of mixed flowers ever since. Everything that has gone before should really be considered only as the preface to the real story. However, we must realize that most of these seventeenth-century arrangements and compositions of flowers and fruits were not literal translations onto canvas of actual bouquets. Many of them were idealized combinations of flowers of all seasons, composed from previous studies rather than an actual model, and displayed with the keenest perception and an inspired feeling for design.

Coupled with the rare ability to capture the palpable loveliness of blossoms was an intense interest in natural science. It must be remembered that this was an age of great scientific discoveries. The intellectual accomplishments that seemed to burst upon the world in the short space of a hundred years between the middle sixteenth century and middle seventeenth century included those of Copernicus and Galileo in the field of astronomy, Pascal, Descartes, and Newton in the field of mathematics, Vesalius and Harvey in the field of medicine, and the Flemish scientist Clusius (the author of *Rarierum Plantarum Historia,* published at Antwerp in 1601) in the field of botany. In the realm of horticulture great strides were made, particularly in Holland and England. Both countries were great seafaring powers whose merchant marines were sailing the seas, trading in remote places, and settling new colonies in the far corners of the earth. From these distant places came

Figure 26. An allegorical representation of Smell. One of a set depicting the five senses by the Flemish engraver, Frans Floris. Flora is shown filling a basket container with all the best-loved garden flowers. This print has added significance, for the bouquet includes two slender tulips, just introduced to the Netherlands. It is about the earliest portrayal of the tulip in northern European records, dating as it does from 1561.

knowledge and actual specimens of such new flowers as *Chrysanthemum sinense,* the so-called African marigold (from Mexico), cactus, cockscomb, nasturtium, and the giant sunflower. Overland from the east had already arrived the tulip, the crown imperial, and the cyclamen from Persia; the common lilac *(Syringa vulgaris)* of the Balkans; and the hyacinth and narcissus from Greece.

Figure 27. "Concordia," a family scene depicting contentment, by Martin de Vos, engraved by Crispin de Passe. The bouquet of flowers is included as a cheerful touch in a happy domestic scene.

Figure 28. An early seventeenth-century painting by Jan "Velvet" Breughel (1568-1625), "The Visit of the Infanta Isabella and the Archduke Albert to the Anti-quary's." The painting, of which this is a detail, includes shells from the Pacific and Turkish carpets which trading ships were bringing home from faraway places during this era of exploration. The large group of flowers shown in the detail includes a giant sunflower from America.

Since tremendous advances had been made in the production of books, this new knowledge of horticulture was soon disseminated. Engraved metal plates now reproduced a specimen in more precise detail than had been possible with the wood block, and illustrations made by this new process or painted by artists served to produce a new type of botanical book, the florilegium. In contrast to the old herbals, which described only useful garden plants, the florilegium displayed flowers because of their beauty as well as their horticultural interest. Many such books were commissioned by wealthy patrons or were published by the botanists themselves.

Growing flowers had become a favorite avocation with many people. By the year 1634, almost every Dutchman was growing tulips which, since their introduction to the Netherlands around 1562, had become of increasing interest because of their tendency to "break." This, as every gardener knows, is the color variation that frequently occurs as flecks and stripes. Now thought to be caused by a virus, these markings were early classified into two groups, the *Bizarres* being the tulips with yellow ground-color and red markings, and the *Bybloems* those with white grounds and rose or purple markings. These variations were unpredictable, so that a true spirit of gambling entered into the production of tulip bulbs. It was a gamble which appealed to rich and poor alike. Speculation ran rife, and "Tulipomania" or the great tulip boom was on. The mad whirl lasted for three years and ended in 1637 with many lost fortunes and a glutted market.

Certainly we no longer have to look far for evidence that cut flowers were indeed taken indoors to be enjoyed. The illustrated group of sixteenth-century engravings starts pointing the way. The artists of this period used flowers in their symbolical representations of the senses, the elements, the seasons, or certain human qualities, all of which provided popular subject matter. We are treated to a real family scene, complete with flowers enlivening the interior, in a picture entitled *Concordia* by Martin de Vos (Fig. 27). Next, let us look at the genre paintings of the following century, which so accurately describe the daily life of the people. Specialized painters like Vermeer or Terborch were concerned

Figure 29. Jan Breughel was the most prolific flower painter of the Flemish school. He was often referred to as "Velvet" Breughel, not because of the texture of his paintings but because of the velvet suits he wore. Here he has made a study of "Flowers in a Delft Vase." The manufacture of Delftware was started soon after the beginning of the seventeenth century, and this vase must have been one of the earliest pieces made.

Figure 30. The ancient mythological story of Pausias (the painter) and Glycera (the garland-maker) is told in a combined painting by Rubens and "Velvet" Breughel. Breughel's flowers tell us much about what was commonly grown in European gardens of this period. (See also figure 31.)

Ringling Museum of Art, Sarasota

more with people than with flowers. Jan Steen, however, shows us that a gay bunch of flowers was an appropriate and natural addition to the life of *A Happy Family* (Fig. 33). In Flanders, Jan Breughel, usually referred to as "Velvet" Breughel, suggested the light and colorful touch flowers can give to an interior when he depicted the antiquary's place of business (Fig. 28), and Van Dyck has shown us just how effective a few choice blooms in a fragile glass vase can be (Fig. 35).

The containers for flowers in this period are of interest, for they show great variety. At first we notice bottle-shaped vessels, jugs and ewers, the objects of ordinary daily use. Soon, however, many beautiful glass shapes appear to display the flowers. There are deep green, knobbed glass vases and goblets which were made in Germany and the Netherlands, as well as the glass that came by sea from Venice. As Holland expanded her empire overseas, Chinese ceramics were imported, and blue and white oriental porcelain became the rage. Soon able Dutch craftsmen developed a cheaper ware, which we know as Delft, in order to help fill the demand for "china" ware. Among the many articles manufactured were flower holders (Fig. 29) and ornamental vases for the mantelpiece known as "garnitures." These were made up in sets of five pieces modeled after Chinese shapes and included three covered jars and two beaker-like vases for holding flowers. By the time the school of flower painting reached its peak in the late seventeenth and early eighteenth century, the classic urn, often seen in terra cotta in the Van Huysum paintings, was the most fitting shape to hold the great profusion of flowering material depicted.

Figure 31. There are at least twenty-five different kinds of garden flowers in this painting by Jan Breughel. The distinctive form of the crown imperial (Fritillaria imperialis), seen at the top of the bouquet, is often shown in a similar position in other Flemish and Dutch paintings.

Left: Figure 32. "Flowers in a Vase," painted in 1627 by the Flemish artist Ambrosius Bosschaert the Elder. The stiff little group of flowers is not gracefully displayed, but the flower content is of interest, as is the glass vase in which it is placed.

Below: Figure 33. "The Happy Family," painted by Jan Steen (1626-1679). Music, flowers, wine, and food are the ingredients of a merry Dutch scene.

Opposite page: Figure 34. One of the most exquisite of all Flemish flower paintings, "Flowers on a Window Sill," by Ambrosius Bosschaert (1614-1654), is beautifully detailed and warm in coloring. There are yellow and red striped tulips, red anemones and ranunculus, a red and white carnation, yellow columbine, iris, narcissus, a fritillary, rose and pink cabbage roses, and an orange marigold from America. Bits of blue are provided by a columbine, an iris, a scilla, and a grape hyacinth.

34

Mauritshuis, The Hague

35

Above: Figure 35. Detail from the "Portrait of Margareta Snyders," by Anthony Van Dyck (1599-1641). Just a few flowers are displayed in a beautiful glass vase.

Below: Figure 36. A charming bouquet painted by Jan van Huysum. This grouping of flowers, with its fine proportions and dominant center of interest, could well find its counterpart in a contemporary arrangement. The predominant colors are rosy red, pink, and white.

Figure 37. "Flowers in a Vase," by Willem van Aelst (1626-1688). The eyes are caught immediately by a strong center of interest — orange marigolds, white guelder-roses, a bright poppy-anemone, and a very large pink cabbage rose. The pale yellow of a sulphur butterfly silhouetted against gray-green poppy foliage effects a subtle transition between the red, orange, and pink. The sky-blue ribbon provides another dominant color note, and the golden metal vase has textural interest. This may truly be called an "arrangement," for there is a studied design. A strong diagonal line starts at the topmost poppy and passes through the marigold and the guelder-roses down through the carnations at left. The oppositional straight line of the marble makes a strong base for a right-angled triangle. The pattern of the outline and the rhythm of the poppy leaves keep the design from being static.

Figure 38. "Vase with Flowers," by the Dutch painter Jan van Huysum (1682-1749), is one of the great masterpieces of flower painting. With a profusion of flowers and fruits, van Huysum so arranged his composition that it is neither massive nor static. The warm orange, yellow, and red-orange hues are in strong contrast with the blue and white, but they are skillfully blended into one beautiful whole by the softening greens and pale pinks and the golden tone of the background.

Figure 39. "Hollyhocks" painted by Jan Van Huysum emphasizes the very great textural interest of foliage. The pale pink blooms set up a large focal area of light values in strong contrast to the vibrant colors of orange marigolds and red poppies.

An even greater variety than in the containers, of course, is seen in the flowering materials which they held and in the fruits which were so frequently arranged with them. Invariably we see the tulip, in its broken colors, and the rose. A single pink rose is sometimes found, but usually the double pink and white forms of the Damask rose (*Rosa Damascena*) and the Cabbage rose (*Rosa centifolia*), as well as the double yellow Sulphur rose (*Rosa hemisphaerica*), are the ones portrayed. There was a great interest in roses in Holland at this time, and it was here that the first roses were grown from seed in Europe.

Peonies and iris probably rank next in interest, the peonies being the double *Paeonia officinalis,* ranging in color from deep rose to white, the iris being of two varieties, bearded or *Germanica,* and bulbous. The yellow and brown *Iris variegata* of central Europe is shown at the very top of Bosschaert's delightful painting (Fig. 34), but usually the colors of the iris are variations of blue, lavender, mauve, and grayed white, *Iris pallida* being one of the parents of the many modern varieties.

Fritillarias, both the guinea-hen flower and the stately crown imperial, lend their distinctive forms to these canvases, and the lily is represented frequently by the white Madonna and by the reddish Martagon or Turkscap lily. Curiously enough one of childhood's favorites, the old-fashioned snowball (*Viburnum opulus sterile*), appears time and time again; it is always referred to as the guelder-rose, since it is said to have originated in the Netherlands province of Gelderland. Both African and French marigolds frequently bring their warm orange hues to these groupings, and as flower painting progressed, the curving stems of poppies provide the artists with baroque curves to add to their rhythmic designs. The word *design* brings us to the real reason for studying these masterpieces.

There is a vast difference between the *bouquet* of flowers that "Velvet" Brueghel (1568-1625) painted (Fig. 31), and the *flower arrangement* of Van Huysum (1682-1749) about a century later (Fig. 38). Brueghel presents a very generous sampling of the garden; all the flowers he could possibly gather are shown here with great fidelity and attention to detail. It positively invites one to identify every flower that makes up the group. Van Huysum on the contrary appeals more to our emotions. There is sensuous beauty in his light falling on translucent petals and reflexed leaves, in his warm colors highlighted by whites and pale pinks, in his free-flowing line and swirling motion. Here we have a chance to study every basic principle taught by today's teachers of flower arrangement. First we look for a design form, and we find that most of these mass arrangements are based on an oval. Starting with the hollyhock tip and the single French marigolds at the top of Van Huysum's famous National Gallery picture in London (Fig. 38), the eyes are carried down on the left by a nodding poppy bud to a large and deeply serrated poppy leaf, examining on the way some narcissus and hyacinths. The eyes travel over the base, past some blue morning glories, and linger over the luscious green grapes and tenderly painted pink roses before being attracted by a low-hanging red peony head, its foliage, and a spray of apple blossoms. Swinging on to the top again we examine some tulips and a stem of pale yellow hollyhocks. All the stems that show in the picture seem to accent this graceful oval form. The flowers leaning and spilling over the edge of the great terra-cotta urn serve both to draw the eye down and around and to divide the canvas into unequal portions. Every art student has at some time learned that it is inadvisable to have the horizon line of a landscape run directly across the middle of a painting and thereby set up two areas of equal size and interest to vie for the onlooker's attention. The student will notice that in not one of the flower paintings by these artists of the Low Countries is the straight line of a container's rim allowed arbitrarily to divide the canvas.

One of the most successful features of the late seventeenth and early eighteenth-century flower paintings of Van Huysum, Margarita Haverman, Rachel Ruysch, and van Brussel is the three dimensional semblance of depth gained by clever side lighting and

Figure 40. The Flemish painter Gasper Pedro Verbruggen (1664-1730) painted this bold and colorful composition of strong reds, yellows, and orange contrasted with violet, blue, pink, and white. Newcomers from Central America, the giant sunflower, the "African" marigold, and nasturtiums are included. On the right is an old garden favorite, "Love-lies-bleeding (Amaranthus caudatus).

particularly by the turning of flower heads. All these painters delighted in revealing the structure of flowers; they have shown us how stems and blossoms join, how beautiful some forms are in profile, and of what great textural interest is foliage. The eye never tires of traveling around, through, and into these lovely bouquets.

Whereas the early paintings were somewhat spotty in their handling of color, the artists of the late period handled color magnificently. There is a rich, warm hue hovering over most of the canvases, yet so much white, pale yellow, and pale pink is mingled with the orange, terra cotta, and mellow reds that a delightful contrast is set up; many dark and light forms are subtly juxtaposed without our eyes having to dart from place to place. All the motion is gradual. Many variations of green are introduced which bring unity to these mixed groupings, and always they are enlivened by little touches of blue. It is a pure Dutch blue. It is Holland's blue skies reflected in the canals of the countryside. It is Delft blue, the blue found in Vermeer's paintings, and the blue of the morning glory we call "heavenly."

Figure 41. "Flower Piece," by Jan van Huysum. One of the delights of this artist's paintings is the inner lighting that seems to emanate from them. The very strong feeling of depth or third dimension is much to be desired in present-day flower arranging. Like many fellow artists, van Huysum turned the heads of flowers to the back or side so their many aspects could be studied.

William Rockhill Nelson Gallery of Art, Kansas City

44

Figure 42. A brilliant canvas painted by P. T. van Brussel in 1790. The primrose Auricula, so beloved by eighteenth-century gardeners, is prominently displayed among the peonies, narcissus, stock, and roses. The broken-stemmed flower at the left is a parrot tulip, and the gray-green leaves which clasp the stem of the opium poppy quickly identify it. They are placed in a terra-cotta vase.

Figure 43. "Still Life," by Jan Van Os (1744-1808). A striking contrast of complementary colors — blue and orange — is skillfully handled in this Dutch painting. In the upper left side of his painting, Van Os has included the delphinium, which was introduced to gardens during the last half of the eighteenth century. The gray-green leaves which clasp the stem of the opium poppy quickly identify it.

Figure 44. There is a feeling of delicacy and grace, and of fine proportion, in this arrangement which is well worth studying. An appropriate choice was made in selecting an urn in which to place the flowers. School of Van Os. Dutch, XVIIIth century.

Figure 45. "Flowers in a Blue Vase," by the Flemish painter Willem van Leen (1753-1825). The flower arranger will immediately notice here the S-curve, described by Hogarth as the "line of beauty." To keep the design from becoming too obvious, the artist introduced the oppositional curve of a tuberose. The pineapple, one of the wonders of the seventeenth and eighteenth centuries, takes its place among the fruit at the base.

Figure 46. An arrangement by the author which was inspired by the old Dutch and Flemish flower paintings. Color, flower content, and the choice of an appropriate vase were the main considerations in assembling this composition. An attempt was made to select types of flowering material grown in the Low Countries during the seventeenth and eighteenth centuries, choosing those which were of the favored colors of the time — warm yellow, orange, red, blue, pale pink, and white.

LE GRAND SIECLE, THE EIGHTEENTH AND EARLY NINETEENTH CENTURIES

WHEREAS LIFE in general revolved around the *bourgeoisie* in the Low Countries, and art was an expression of their daily lives, in France all attention in the seventeenth and eighteenth centuries was focused on the court, first that of Louis XIV, then of his successors. Every aspect of cultural life was inextricably tied up with what the king and his courtiers were doing or thinking. The arts did not serve the people, but the court; they were an expression first of the luxury and Baroque magnificence of the aristocracy, and later of its frivolity and fashionable Rococo taste. Under royal patronage, however, all the decorative arts flourished.

For the Gobelin and Beauvais tapestry works, top-ranking artists, including Watteau, Fragonard, and Boucher, were secured as designers. Madame de Pompadour, Louis XV's mistress, became an enthusiastic and intelligent patroness of the arts; she encouraged the granting of royal subsidies to the Sèvres porcelain factory and the Lyons silk industry. She furthered archaeology by furnishing funds for excavations at Herculaneum and Pompeii. When she became interested in the China trade, she started a vogue for chinoiseries in many branches of the applied arts.

When Louis XIV (1643-1715), variously referred to as *Le Grand Monarque* and *Le Roi Soleil,* first began to establish the most magnificent court in all Europe, he very wisely appointed Colbert as finance minister, Le Nôtre as master designer of the gardens, and Charles Le Brun, the most important French painter of the day, as director of all the interior decoration at Versailles. He it was who "discovered" Jean Baptiste Monnoyer (1634-1699). Having painted in the Flemish tradition before he arrived in Paris, Monnoyer was soon commissioned by LeBrun to paint flowers for Gobelin tapestry designs. He was also active in providing painted floral decorations for the rooms of private residences, and ultimately became justly famous for his portfolio of beautiful engravings called *Le Livre de Toutes Sortes de Fleurs d'après Nature.* These plates accurately show the flowers from a horticultural point of view, yet in the true artistic spirit of the time they are displayed so gracefully and with such a feeling for decorative design that they had a great deal of influence on the patterns of textiles and wallpapers in the following century. From our point of view these prints are interesting for the light touch they reveal in the display of many flowers. These bouquets give the effect of mass arrangements and yet are never massive. Distinctive forms, gracefully curving stems, and clearly defined outline areas of varied shapes delight the eye, and one feels sure their prototypes in living plant material would very appropriately grace splendid interiors embellished with elaborate wood carving and gold decoration.

An interesting comparison in the handling of subject matter can be made between the engravings of Monnoyer and the paintings of his contemporaries in the Netherlands. An examination of a painting (Frontispiece) by Nicholas Vereendael, whose dates (1640-1691) pretty well coincide with Monnoyer's, will serve to show how different in feeling was the approach of each artist. Of course, since he was painting in oils, Vereendael could depend on shimmering color to gain his effects, whereas the engraver had to depend on free-flowing line; but the difference between the two lies even deeper, in their spirit.

Left: Figure 47. Engraving by Jean Baptiste Monnoyer (1634-1699) from "Livre de Toutes Sortes de Fleurs d'Après Nature." This design has a distinctly French elegance and formality that is accented by the classic container. Of particular interest is the stalk of Gladiolus byzantinus, native to the Mediterranean region.

Collection: Mrs. Roy Arthur Hunt

Figure 48. The sweeping curves of the tuberose and the vase handle endow this engraving with an undeniable French baroque feeling. A hundred years later a Flemish painter, Van Leen, deliberately copied the tuberose and the iris in his "Flowers in a Blue Vase," Fig. 45.

The Pierpont Morgan Library

Figure 49. "Flowers in a Gilded Urn," by Jean Baptiste Monnoyer. This mass arrangement could never be mistaken for one painted by a Dutch or Flemish artist of the period, for there are certain salient features—the paneled background, the lack of still-life accessories, the color harmonies —that stamp it as definitely French.

It is of interest to us, as flower arrangers, to notice at this time the introduction of the gladiolus and the snapdragon, which have not appeared in any earlier source material examined so far. Monnoyer shows us the *Gladiolus byzantinus* (Fig. 47) known as the corn lily in the Mediterranean region where it grows. This has dark purple flowers with a white central line marking the lower segments; another early variety was white-flowered. Neither of these was as showy as the South African varieties we know today. The snapdragon in the little bouquet (Fig. 51) is the common *Antirrhinum majus,* with a color range from purple to red to white.

The opulent court life of *le grand siècle,* as the period of Louis XIV's reign was called, with all its grandiose trappings, was played out in settings in the grand manner. The rooms at Versailles were large in scale, decorated with elaborate wood and stone carvings; they had marble fireplaces, parquetry and marble floors, and many painted mural decorations. Mirrors and gilding added to the lavishness. Decorative flower arrangements, large in scale, provided further embellishment, and we have a chance to see just how they

Figure 50. A basket of flowers designed and engraved by Monnoyer.

Opposite page, top: Figures 51 and 52. Two little bouquets designed and engraved by Monnoyer. One includes snapdragon; the other, a lily, a daffodil, and lily-of-the-valley. Figure 53. XVIIth-century Gobelin tapestry depicting a reception given by Louis XIV for a Spanish ambassador. Note the flowers in the long row of pedestal-supported urns against the wall.

Figure 52

Pierpont Morgan Library, New York

Figure 51

Figure 53

Musée de Versailles

Figure 54. Trompe l'oeil painting on the Queen's staircase, Chateau de Versailles. See description below.

were used by examining the large painting, still in place today, on the Queen's staircase (Fig. 54). This is a clever piece of *trompe l'oeil* (eye deceiving) painting, as the marble balustrade is real and the canvas begins just above it. The attendant, dressed *à la Turque,* slips a strong-stemmed tulip in place, while another attendant appears with more flowers. The large metal urn is typical of the period; it is similar to the hundreds of enormous classic marble urns which decorate the formal gardens of the palace.

A Gobelin tapestry (Fig. 53) which portrays an audience given by Louis gives us further insight into how the rooms were decorated with flowers. Not only do we see a potted tree, very likely an orange, but along the wall we notice a row of pedestal-supported vases of flowers. Anyone who has ever been to Versailles will remember the enormous conservatory known as *l'orangerie.* Here, most of the approximately 3000 orange trees which were displayed in the gardens during the summer, were cared for during the winter months. Others, placed in silver tubs or marble urns decorated the Hall of Mirrors and the State Apartments. It seems quite within the realm of possibility that other flowering material was raised in this huge conservatory all year round for the decoration of the palace. We do know positively that during the outdoor growing season, quantities of flowers to be used in decoration as well as millions of plants to fill the elaborate parterre gardens were grown in a vast kitchen and cutting garden. The large kitchen garden had to supply food for thousands. At the Grand Trianon were another *orangerie,* hot houses, and a nursery which supplied its justly famous gardens with continuously changing pots of narcissus, hyacinths, lilies, heliotrope, jasmine, tuberoses, and carnations.

Blain de Fontenay, who painted the flowers seen in the picture on the Queen's staircase, shows us in another painting (Fig. 55) an elaborate arrangement in a gilded metal container set on a console table which is characteristic of the period. Desportes, another

54

popular still-life painter, placed his flowers in a bronze urn of Renaissance inspiration (Fig. 56), a type which we have seen before in the staircase painting. His arrangement is realistic in its lack of exaggerated curves and the colors are ably distributed. The painting is decidedly French in feeling; it lacks the warm golden tones of the late Flemish period. The combination of blue, lavender, pink, and small bits of yellow with rich red tones keeps it from being insipid.

The sumptuousness of royal living is reflected in the portrait of Louis XV's wife, Marie Leczinska (Fig. 57). Dressed in a flower-strewn brocade, with an ermine-trimmed court train of royal blue and gold, she holds in her hand a sprig of jasmine, ready to add it to the roses and carnations already placed in a precious vase of crystal with gold mountings. Another crystal vase is included in Marie Antoinette's portrait (Fig. 60).

With the end of the Sun King's reign in 1715, there was a shifting of emphasis from Versailles to the more intimate setting of the salons and boudoirs of the aristocracy. It

Figure 55. "The Bust of Louis XIV," painted by Blain de Fontenay (1653-1715). Lilacs, double-flowering cherry, and guelder-roses (the "snowball" viburnum) are combined with tulips and roses in a magnificent gilded vase placed on a marble console. The lavishness of the arrangement suggests a royal setting.

Photo: Vizzavona *The Louvre, Paris*

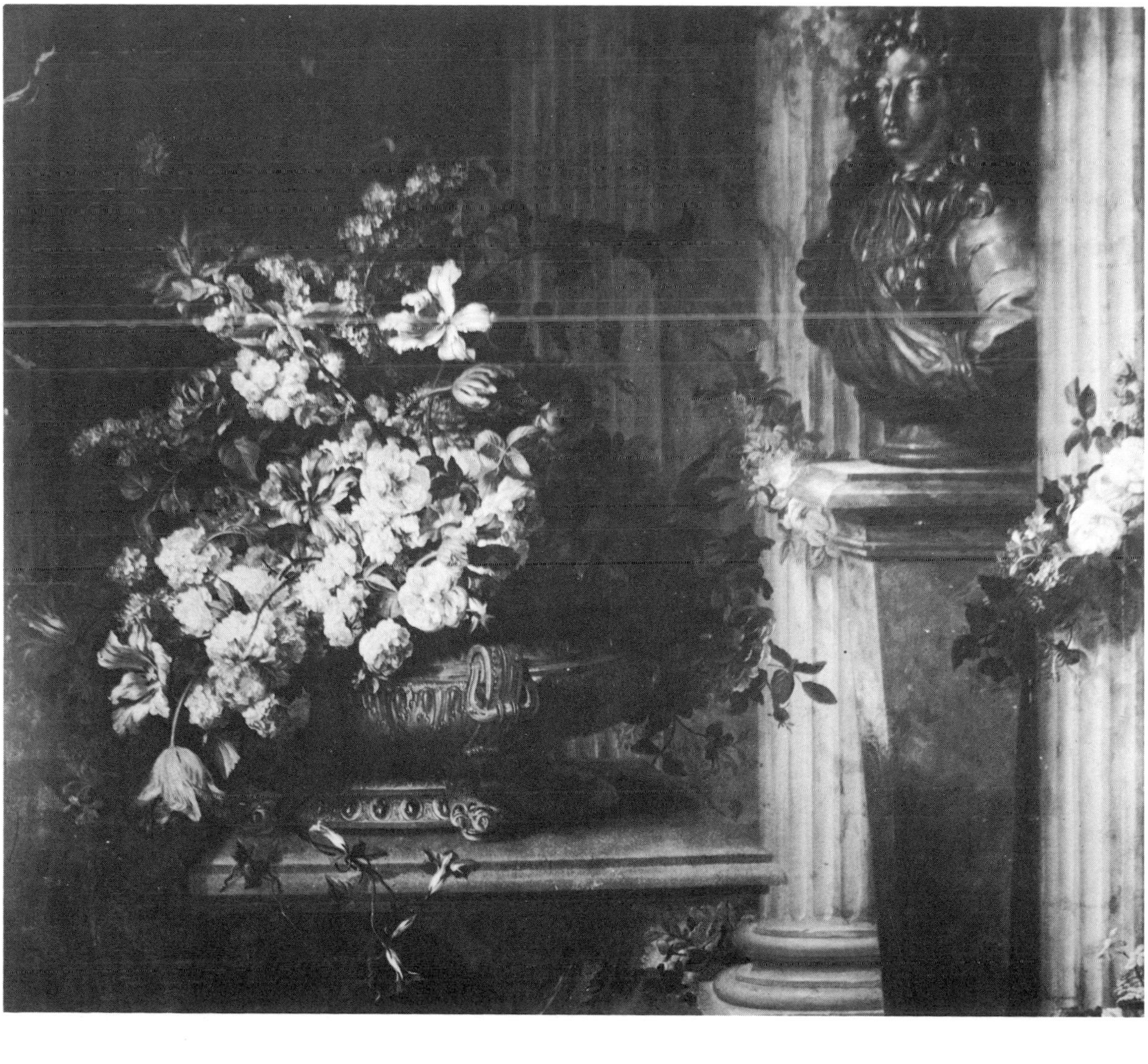

Figure 56. "Flowers in a Vase," painted by A. F. Desportes in 1715. In the great bronze urn lilacs are combined with larkspur and tulips. Within the composition the very double blossoms of flowering cherry create an important area of light tonal interest reiterated by the tazetta narcissus resting on the table.

Figure 57. Detail from the portrait of Marie Leczinska, the wife of Louis XV, painted by Charles Amédée Philippe Van Loo (1715-1795). The queen adds a sprig of jasmine to the flowers already in place in the gold-mounted crystal vase.

was the city of Paris that now became the political and social center of France. This is a period in history when women wielded an enormous "power behind the throne," when their brilliant and witty salons helped shape the thought of the day, and when all forms of art seemed to express femininity. The fashions, the foibles, the feminine frivolities are all recorded for us in drawings and engravings. More realistic in their portrayal of daily life than the fashionable idyllic paintings of Boucher and Fragonard, they are invaluable in a study of the manners and customs of a society hastening to its end.

In the charming rooms of the eighteenth century flowers very frequently were placed on mantels, console tables, and pedestals. The lilac, only occasionally found in Flemish and Dutch flower pieces, was now commonplace, and roses as always seemed to be the most beloved flower. In combination with larkspur, anemones, poppies, and a variety of other soft-hued flowers, they found a congenial setting where the favored colors were light green, pink, rose, mauve, yellow, variations of blue, and warm tones of gray. The flowers were placed in vases, bowls, and baskets.

A number of French potteries besides Sèvres were active in turning out both decorative and functional vases. Many had holes in their tops for keeping flowers in place. Vases of repoussé metal were used, as well as Chinese vases fitted with ormolu mountings. In accordance with the taste for over-ornamentation, oriental porcelains, apparently admired for their color and rarity, yet too refined in their simple outlines for the prevailing taste of the moment, were often mounted in ormolu (bronze gilded with gold leaf) and thus given the popular Rococo curves and motifs (Fig. 70). Some Chinese celadons were even transformed into elaborate ewers with the addition of handles, spouts, and bases.

The outstanding painter who recorded in color some of the beautiful floral combinations was Gerard van Spaëndonck (1746-1822). A Dutchman and a follower of Van Huysum, he came to Paris and taught classes in flower painting at *Le Jardin du roi,* later renamed *Le Jardin des plantes.* Many of his pupils became famous in their own right, notably Pierre Joseph Redouté (1759-1840), of rose fame. Van Spaëndonck's own engraved

Figure 60. Portrait of Marie Antoinette by Mme. Vigée Le Brun, painted about 1785. The beautiful crystal vase, which is mounted in gold, holds a lovely assortment of garden flowers. The lilac has always been especially beloved by the French people.

Left: Figure 61. "Vase of Flowers," by Anne Vallayer-Coster (1744-1818). A natural, informal bouquet of flowers in a deep-azure vase. The blue is repeated in a slender stalk of delphinium; but it is the crispness of the ranunculus and anemone petals, the pale pinks and yellow, and the one glowing red flower at the container's rim that make this canvas unforgettable.

Paul Cailleux Collection, Paris
Photo: Vizzavona

Mme. Poetzsche Collection, Paris
Photo: Caisse Nationale des Monuments Historiques

Right: Figure 62. Another beautiful "Vase of Flowers," painted by Anne Vallayer-Coster in 1789. This informal grouping is shown in a glass pitcher or vase.

Figure 63. Gerard van Spaëndonck painted this beautiful basket of flowers in 1785. It hangs today in Napoleon's apartments at Fontainebleau. A Dutch painter who found favor at the court of Louis XVI, van Spaëndonck was a pupil of van Huysum. He was versatile and was as well known for his botanical illustrations as for his decorative paintings. The classic idea, popular in the late eighteenth century, is evident here; but the typical French coloring of the period and the array of garden flowers remain as before.

Left: Figure 64. Painted design for a tapestry panel. Period of Louis XVI. There are pink, blue, and mauve flowers throughout the panel; red poppies enliven it.

Below: Figure 65. For this arrangement in the French manner, a copy of a Sèvres urn was chosen to hold flowers typical of eighteenth-century France. Lilacs, roses, anemones, stock, and the rococo line of a naturally curving parrot tulip were selected as being particularly appropriate. Arranged by the author.

Photo: Roche

Above: Figure 66. "Vase of Flowers," by Antoine Berjon, 1813. Above, right: Figure 67. "The Broken Tuberose," by Jan Frans Van Dael, 1809. Two flower paintings of the Empire period when classicism was in vogue. The bouquets are familiar, but the marble and alabaster vases add a new note.

Right: Figure 68. Over the centuries and in different countries the humble tumbler has held informal little bouquets. It is seen in medieval illuminations (Fig. 13) and in eighteenth-century portraits (Fig. 104). Detail from "The Messenger," an early XIXth-century painting by Martin Drolling.

work and painted vellums are among the world's finest botanical illustrations. The painting (Fig. 63) which hangs at Fontainebleau, in one of the rooms of Napoleon's suite, gives us a very clear idea of the trend in color and the flower favorites of 1785, when it was painted. Pinks, blues, mauve, soft red, green, and white, combine to produce a very different effect from the flower paintings of the Netherlands, which included so many yellow, orange, and gold tones.

Before the eighteenth century ended, a notable woman painter, Anne Vallayer-Coster (1744-1818) was vying with Chardin for top honors in still-life painting. The bouquets in her canvases (Figs. 61 and 62) were disarmingly simple, but each flower was so knowingly placed and the color so luminous that the canvases hardly seem to belong to the period. One who did not know her dates might well place her work a hundred years later.

We cannot truthfully say that any different style of arranging flowers, other than the bouquet style, emerged from the Neo-classic period which included both the Directoire (1794-1804) and the Empire (1804-1815). Nor did there seem to be any new plant introductions popularized to the extent of being included in decorative paintings or fashion plates. Botanical prints of the first quarter of the nineteenth century, however, do include such newcomers from Africa, South America, and Mexico as *agapanthus* (blue lily-of-the-Nile), *browalia, strelitzia* and the zinnia (known only in its small, rosy-red and violet forms). These tropical curiosities, however, should not be taken as typical of the period.

What had been a trend in the seventeenth century and a *fait accompli* in the eighteenth now reached its culmination in the early nineteenth century. The private botanical garden of rare shrubs, flowers, and trees satisfied the scientific urge of a society that was fashionably interested in the theories of Jean Jacques Rousseau, who had preached the doctrine of a return to the simple pleasures of Nature as a cure for the formalities and sophistication of court society. Royalty and aristocrats, as well as *nouveaux riches,* indulged in this extravagance, employing botanists to gather, gardeners to cultivate, and artists to record their collections. One of the most important of these gardens was that of the Empress Josephine at Malmaison. There she specialized in roses, attempting to grow all the known kinds. Her official flower artist was Redouté, immortalized by over a thousand paintings of roses, eight volumes of lily portraits, and by his invention of a method of color printing.

If flower styles did not change, we know that vases did. Interest in Pompeii during the closing years of the previous century had started a trend toward classicism. This, coupled with Napoleon's desire to emulate Caesar, fostered a very decided change in decorating styles; the antiquities of Greece, Rome, and Egypt being used as models for furniture and ornaments. Ceramic vases were patterned after severely classic urns, with or without handles (Fig. 77), and marble and alabaster vases were not uncommon (Fig. 66). The cornucopia was a favored motif, and the form is often seen terminating in a ram's head of ormolu. One of the busiest places of manufacture of ornamental porcelain vases was the Sèvres factory. Pairs of vases with royal blue, turquoise blue, and emerald green ground colors, hand painted with charming flowers and scenes, were turned out by the thousands in all sizes. The intense, pure hues were well attuned to the favored colors used in newly decorated rooms where a choice of reds, strong greens, purples, brilliant blues, and golden yellow provided striking contrasts with dark mahogany furniture.

Several series of engravings of the early years of the nineteenth century provide us with delightfully entertaining source material for the modes and manners of the time. Both *Le Bon genre,* subtitled *Observations sur les modes et les usages de Paris,* and *Meubles et objets de gout* show the very latest fashions in clothes, furniture, customs and, as the title of one suggests, "tasteful objects." The reader will notice several pieces of furniture which include planting boxes as part of their design. Since they all seem to

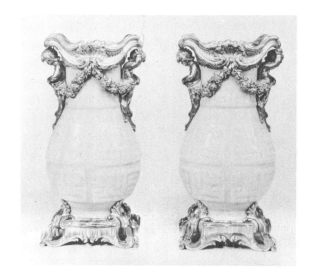

A group of XVIIIth-century French vases. Above, left: Figure 69. Sèvres porcelain jardinière, one of a set of three pieces intended for mantelpiece or dining table. Above, right: Figure 70. Chinese celadon vases mounted in ormolu, or gilded bronze. Period of Louis XV. Right: Figure 71. Soft-paste porcelain vase. Vincennes, circa 1750. Left: Figure 72. Polychrome vase. Sceaux, 1753-1795. Below, right: Figure 73. St. Clement faïence vase, circa 1750.

Figure 75. XVIIIth-century Sèvres porcelain urn with painted decoration by Dodin, after designs by Moreau le Jeune. Pink, blue, and mauve flowers predominate, but a few red poppies enliven the color scheme.

Top left: Figure 74. Hard-paste porcelain vase. Paris, Rue Thiroux, 1788-1800. Center left: Figure 76. Painted porcelain vase, XIXth century. Make unknown. Right: Figure 77. Porcelain vases made in Paris, circa 1800-1825.

display cut flowers instead of plants, the author wonders if these were not meant to be filled with damp sand into which short stems of hardy greens such as arbor vitae might be fixed and fresh flowers added. This is a method described at a later date in both *Godey's Lady's Book* and in an English book called *Floral World and Garden Guide*. The latter recommended growing *lycopodiums* (ground pine) in moist, sandy peat, as a "groundwork for flowers." In the examples illustrated it will be seen how the flowers served to soften the severe lines of classic furniture. In fact, there is something here that presages the Victorian era.

Figure 78. "Flower Arrangement in a Basket," by Antoine Chazal, circa 1820. This artist was one of Van Spaëndonck's pupils, and there are several points of similarity between this engraving and the painting by the latter artist shown on page 61. The informal basket bouquet forms a decided contrast with the classic vase on its pedestal.

Above: Figure 79. Wallpaper panel for a fireboard. French, circa 1825-1830. The ceramic vase is typical of this period.

Left and below: Figures 80 and 81. Illustrations from a series of French engravings called "Meubles et Objets de Goût," published in Paris by La Mésangère. The console (1813) and the plant stand (1820) had planting boxes incorporated in their design. It is apparent, however, that fresh cut flowers were meant to be inserted among the greens.

THE ENGLISH TRADITION

Few PEOPLE in the world have loved flowers and gardens as much as the British. It is a tradition that goes far back in their history, as far back as the Middle Ages. In England during those troublous times, it was not the monks alone who kept small, walled gardens in which to grow plants and small trees, but home owners in general had what would now be called kitchen gardens attached to their houses, though it was not yet customary to have "pleasure gardens." Within these gardens were grown a few simple flowers, such as marigolds, violets, roses, iris, and primroses. These were used for home-made medicines and cosmetics, for flavoring, and even for food, salads or "sallets" in particular. Cut flowers, it seems, were used for making garlands and chaplets, just as in the days of ancient Greece and Rome, and in old illustrated manuscripts one sees women and their maidens making and weaving them. These were also used for church ritual, and it is known that the clergy wore crowns of flowers in processions.

The fifteenth and sixteenth centuries saw the real development of flower gardening, for it was no longer necessary to live behind walls for protection, and castle moats were soon outmoded. The fortress town had given way to individual homes, and Tudor and Elizabethan architecture was the result. These homes included lawns, kitchen gardens, and pleasure gardens. The latter were purely decorative and included knot gardens of clipped box or other low-growing shrubs, filled in with seasonal flowers; there were also *allées*, or covered walks, formed by arching the branches of trees, or by growing over arbors such climbing plants as roses, jasmine, honeysuckle, and rosemary. Topiary work added interest and height variation.

It was considered important to grow fragrant flowers and herbs, for it was thought that their perfume would clear the air of pestilence, and it was also customary to add the agreeable-smelling clippings from the knot edgings to the rushes strewn over the floors of the house. In 1560, a Dutchman, Levinus Lemnius, visited England and wrote a well known description of English homes and hospitality: "Their chambers and parlours strawed over with sweet herbs refreshed mee; their noesgays finely intermingled with sundry sorts of fragraunte flowers, in their bed-chambers and privy rooms, with comfortable smell cheered me up, and entirely delyghted all my senses." Comparing England with Holland he went on to say: "Altho we do trimme up our parlours with greene boughes, freshe herbes or vine leaves, no nation does it more decently, more trimmely, nor more sightly than they doe in Englande."

One wonders just how the custom of filling the fireplaces with greens or flowers started, for another visitor to England describes how holly was used for this purpose "from Good Friday until All Hallows Day" during the months when heat was not needed in the living rooms. It was a decorative custom that lingered on, for eighteenth century paintings prove that it was quite usual then, and today's visitors to England will find the custom still prevailing.

During the time of the first Elizabeth, as well as that of her father, Henry VIII, more and more interest was taken in flowers, and varieties new to the English were brought over by Protestant Flemish refugees escaping from the persecution of the Spaniards. It is thought that they brought with them the carnation, which was soon to be called the gillyflower.[1] It is known these same Protestant refugees introduced the auricula (*Primula auricula*), often referred to as Bear's ears because of the texture of its leaves; and of course the tulip and narcissus came with them too. They also brought along a more advanced knowledge of gardening practices.

At about this period, two books made their appearance which forever stand as milestones along the garden path—John Gerarde's *Herball*, first published in London in 1597, and John Parkinson's *Paradisi In Sole Paradisus Terrestris* (Park-in-sun's Earthly Paradise), 1629. Both men were physicians, botanists, and the owners of fine gardens. The frontispiece of the 1636 edition of Gerarde's *Herball* is of interest (Fig. 84), for it shows two flower arrangements made up of many garden favorites and some of the flowers which Parkinson referred to as "outlandish." Parkinson described these as "being strangers unto us, and giving the beauty and bravery of their colours so early before many of our owne

[1] The carnation (*Dianthus caryophyllus*) is named for the clove tree (*karyophyllum* in Greek). To a number of flowers whose fragrance resembles clove the name gillyflower has been given. This seems to be derived from the old French word for clove, *gilofre*. Carnations, pinks, Sweet William, stock, rocket, and wallflowers have all been called gillyflowers, but the names are usually modified in some way. Thus stock is called stock gillyflower, Dame's rocket is Queen's gillyflower, and clove pinks are clove gillyflowers. The carnation (called by Parkinson *Caryophyllus maximus*), long cultivated out of doors in Europe, seems always to have retained its own name, but all the many other varieties of *Dianthus caryophyllus* seem generally to be called just gillyflowers, gilloflowers, or gilliflowers.

Figure 82. Portrait of the German merchant, George Gisze, painted by Hans Holbein in 1532. Both painter and sitter came to London during the Reformation. Carnations had been newly introduced to England by refugee Flemings, but their popularity became such that Parkinson, a hundred years later, wrote of them: "carnations and gilloflowers bee the chiefest flowers of account in all our English gardens."

Figure 83. The family of Sir Thomas More, painted by Hans Holbein about the year 1530. Here are lilies, carnations, iris, columbine, and peonies from a Tudor garden.

bred flowers, the more to entice us to their delight." Among those he mentioned were "Daffodils, Fritillarias, Iacinthes, Saffron-flowers, Lilies, Flowerdeluces, Tulipas, Anemones, French Cowslips or Beare's eares, White and Yellow Jasmine, Cyclamen, Muscari, Christmas rose, Double red ranunculous, Double Hollyhock, Yellow Larkes spurre, Oleander, Bellflowers of many kinds, Pyracantha or Prickly Corall."

Yellow Larkes spurre or Larkes heeles was the *Nasturtium Indicum.* Parkinson wrote that it "hath a fine, small sent, very pleasing, which being placed in the middle of some carnations or gilloflowers make a delicate Tussimussie, as they call it, or Nosegay, for sight and sent." It is Parkinson who tells us so many little things about cut flowers. He lets us know that they were taken indoors and placed in vases when he says of daffodils, "Many are so exceeding sweete that a very few are sufficient to perfume a whole chamber." He says of the wallflower, "The sweetnesse of the flowers causeth them to be generally used in Nosegayes, and to deck up houses"; and of the Flagge (German iris), "It well doth serve to decke up both a Garden and House with natures beauties." Of thrift, which he recommends for the edging of the knot garden, he writes that it "will grow bushie and thicke" if cut with "a paire of garden sheeres." In the summertime it will "send forth many short stalkes of pleasant flowers, to decke up an house among other sweete herbes." These refer-

71

Figure 84. Detail from the title page of the 1636 edition of John Gerarde's "Herball." Many European flowers which Parkinson referred to as "outlandish" had now become a familiar part of the English scene. The vases are of added interest, for they are similar to the one shown in the Hollar engraving, "Spring."

ences to the flowers which were cut and used as decoration indoors are numerous, and we get the feeling that todays glorious bouquets from English gardens had their antecedents here. Always there was an emphasis on fragrance. At a banquet at which Edward Sackville, fourth Earl of Dorset, was host, on July 3, 1636, the servants were ordered "to perfume the room often in the meal with orange flower water upon a hot pan. To have fresh bowls in every corner and flowers tied upon them, and sweet briar, stock, gilly-flowers, pinks, wall-flowers and any other sweet flowers in glasses and pots in every window and chimney." This quotation is of further interest in that it gives us an idea of where flowers were usually placed at a time in which occasional furniture was scarce, benches and tables being the most necessary and most frequently used items.

A lovely perfume must surely have emanated from all the flowers engraved by Wenceslaus Hollar in his picture of Spring. No one could be more natural or more charming than that lady of the time of Charles the First, pictured adding tulips to her bouquet which must surely have been picked in the formal garden we glimpse in Figure 85. Please note that, since she is representing Spring, her furs are about to be packed away! The date is 1641, and among her flowers are to be seen the guelder-rose (snowball), the German bearded iris, the Madonna lily, the tulip, and the rose.

Hampton Court very certainly made use of cut flowers for decoration, for among its collections are some Delft hyacinth and tulip vases which we suppose must frequently have been in use and must have pleased the reigning sovereigns of the end of the seventeenth century, the Dutch William and his wife Mary. These containers are extremely large and ornate, rather similar to the one shown (Fig. 84). There are a number of upward-tilting spouts for holding flowers in place, or through which bulbs could sprout if they were started in water. One set of vases, pagoda-like in shape, consisted of a number of water trays, graduated in size, which were stacked one on top of the other. When filled with gay tulips these typically Delft blue and white pieces must have been extremely striking. Pyramids of color were thereby introduced into dark apartments.

All during the seventeenth century, just as in the Netherlands and in France during this great age of exploration and expansion, foreign plants in increasing numbers reached England. Since many of the imported plants were tender, conservatories and hothouses

Figure 85. "Spring," one of a set of engravings showing the four seasons. The artist, Wenceslaus Hollar, was a Czechoslovak who, for forty years, lived in London. This engraving was done in 1641. The little verse which accompanies it begins: "Furrs fare you well, the Winter is quite gone, And beauty's quarter now is coming on."

Figure 86. Delft tulip vase, circa 1700.

Opposite page: Figure 87. The month of June from "Twelve Months of Flowers," published by Robert Furber, designed by Peter Casteels, and engraved by H. Fletcher, 1730.

Danish Museum of Decorative Arts, Copenhagen

gradually appeared and were to become a necessity for the country gentleman of the next century. On the ships of The East India Company, voyagers sent home such things as the tobacco plant of Virginia, the century plant (agave), and potatoes from the Americas. Queen Mary collected "exoticks" for the hothouses at Hampton Court, and no expense was spared in her collecting of rare plants from other parts of the world.

By 1730, when Robert Furber published his famous *Twelve Months of Flowers,* twenty-five of our American plants were included. These well-known prints formed a catalog by means of which people could order the seeds, plants, or bulbs of the flowers represented, for Furber was a nurseryman. A Flemish artist, Pieter Casteels, made the original paintings, which were then engraved by Fletcher. The prints suggest large and colorful mass arrangements, tastefully designed, but since the flowers are all one of a kind, their greatest value lies in what they have to tell us about the available flowering material at the beginning of the Georgian period. The most popular flower seems to have been the *Auricula,* a *Primula* of velvety perfection, of beautiful color and with prominent markings. We have seen it conspicuously displayed in the Dutch, Flemish, and French flower arrangements of both the seventeenth and eighteenth centuries. Twenty-six named varieties, mostly in variations of maroon and violet, can be counted, while nineteen varieties of the anemone occur, in double and single forms, in the following colors: red, purple, blue, rose and white. Blue and white hyacinths both single and double, early and late, are shown in about a dozen varieties. Fourteen roses and eleven tulips are listed. From this it is a fair supposition that a very great interest in gardening existed. This was manifested, for example, in the simple practice of potting up plants to be enjoyed indoors. We catch glimpses of them in paintings and engravings, and read such references to the practice as this: "Carnations cultivated in pots are proper ornamental plants for adorning the more conspicuous places about the house." Elsewhere we read: "The plants of the steeple bell-flower (*Campanula pyramidalis*) are trained for adorning halls and chimneys." Mignonette is recommended to be grown in pots, "Since it's fragrance may be conveyed

74

1 Perennian dwarf Sun flow:
  Ultramarine & Prußian.
2 blew Iris Major
  Blew Nigella or
3 Fennel flower.
4 Moon Trefoile
5 Upright Sweet William.
6 Saxifrage.
7 Cinque-foile.

8 Pansies or Hearts-ease.
9 Maidens blush Rose.
10 Yellow Jasmine.
11 Blew Corn flower.
12 Blush Belgick Rose.
13 The Francford Rose.
14 Double Martagan.
15 Orchis or Bee flower.
16 Scarlet Lotutea.

JUNE

17 Fraxinella.
18 Moß province Rose.
19 Double Virginian silk Graß
20 White Rose.
21 Dutch hundred leav'd Rose
22 White Batchellers Button
23 Rosa Mundi.
24 Mountain Lychnis.
25 Dwarf Iris strip'd.

26 White Jasmine.
27 Scarlet Geranium.
28 Yellow Martegon.
29 Red Martegon.
30 Teucrium or Germander.
31 Mountain dwarf Pink
32 Yellow Corn Marygold.
33 Purple sweet Pea.
34 Greek Valerian.

Printed for John Bowles at the Black Horse in Cornhill

J. Clark Sculp.

Above, left: Figure 88. Salt-glazed Staffordshire stoneware. One of a pair of wall vases. 1750-1760. Above, right: Figure 89. Turquoise-colored soft-paste Chelsea porcelain. 1760-1765.

Left: Figure 90. Detail from "The Lady's Last Stake," by William Hogarth (1697-1764). The paired bouquets on the mantelpiece are a realistic, homelike touch.

Opposite page, lower left: Figure 92. Blue Wedgwood jasper-ware flower holder with perforated top. In a Wedgwood catalogue mention is made of flower holders for the table "both for roots and the dressing with flowers." (At that time the word roots was used to designate bulbs.) Opposite page, lower right: Figure 93. Chelsea porcelain vase with perforated top for holding flowers.

Right: Figure 91. Detail from a painting by Gawen Hamilton entitled "The Vicar of the Parish at the House of the Infant Squire." This little conversation piece shows the old English custom of filling the fireplace with flowers during the months when heat was unnecessary. The flower-filled containers are always referred to as "bough-pots."

Photo: A. C. Cooper   Collection: Sir Alec Martin

Metropolitan Museum of Art

to the parlour of the recluse or the chamber of the valetudinarian." When one recalls how cool are the rooms of houses heated only by fireplaces and grates, one does not wonder that these plants thrived.

References to flower bouquets are not at all unusual in English writings of the eighteenth century. Long-lasting dried bouquets were made by the ladies, and Philip Miller,[2] a contemporary of Robert Furber, wrote that the flowering heads of the globe amaranth (Gomphrena globosa) "are beautiful, and if gathered before they are too far advanced, retain their beauty several years." Listed in an early volume of Curtis's Botanical Magazine, during the last decade of the eighteenth century, is statice, or purple thrift. Of this plant it is said, "The dried flowers are a pretty ornament for the mantelpiece in the winter."

It is a certainty that bunches of fresh flowers graced the English drawing rooms so beautifully furnished with mahogany furniture by Chippendale, Hepplewhite, and Sheraton, along with oriental rugs, silk hangings, and imported wallpapers. We pick up bits of information from the botanical authors such as Miller, as they go about describing all the cultivated flowers. For instance, of Aconitum or monkshood he says, "It is cultivated for the Beauty of its long spikes of blue flowers, which are brought to the markets in London, toward the end of May, when it commonly flowers; so that these being intermixed with the Guelder roses and other flowers of the same season, make an agreeable variety when properly blended, to adorn Halls and other Apartments."

Flower vases, as well as ornamental vases for decoration only, were made in quantity by the busy British ceramic manufacturers. All the well known factories where pottery and porcelain were made, those of Wedgwood, Chelsea, Worcester, Bristol, and Rockingham, to name but a few, were busy turning out not only dinnerware and ornaments, but vases. Many of these were fashioned with ingenious holes and openings to hold the flowers in place (Figs. 92 and 93). The visitor at Williamsburg will see authentic antique vases such as these in use, and at Winterthur a pair of Chinese Lowestoft vases with similar openings is on exhibition. The Chelsea porcelain factory also produced charming and expensive porcelain flowers which had ormolu stems. These artificial flowers were meant to be used in vases when real ones were unavailable.

It seems strange that so few artists were interested in including flower bouquets in portraits, for we know bouquets to have been a prominent part of the English domestic scene. We may search through the numerous portraits by Gainsborough, Romney, and Reynolds, but not a vase of flowers is to be seen. Then we realize that most portrait backgrounds are landscapes, and we recall that a tremendous change had taken place in gardening itself. Many of the fashionable people who were painted had succumbed to the very fashionable trend of having gardens in the "landscape style."

Ever since Henry the Eighth's time, all gardens (except those of the cottager) had been laid out in formal beds. Allées, canals, parterres (beds laid out in elaborate patterns), and terraces made up the garden. Whether in Holland, in France, or in England, the same type prevailed on a larger or smaller scale. Topiary art, described by Addison in The

2 Philip Miller, (1691–1771), English author of The Gardener's Dictionary, first published in London between the years 1731–39. Miller describes himself on the title page of his dictionary as "Gardener to the Worshipful Company of Apothecaries in their Botanick Garden in Chelsea." This important and popular work went into nine editions. A number of abridged editions were published also. The sixth edition, brought out in 1752 made use of the Linnean system of nomenclature.

Opposite page: Figure 94. "The Painter's Wife" (Detail), by Allan Ramsay, showing pink and yellow roses arranged in a large blue and white earthenware vase.

Figure 95. King George III, Queen Charlotte, and six of their children, painted by John Zoffany in 1771. A profusion of garden flowers fills an ornate vase in a regal setting.

Spectator as "trees rising in cones, globes and pyramids," became overdone. Finally, by mid-century, there was a decided reaction against such formalities. Since gardens had been planned in the same way for so long, it was natural that when the reaction came it was a violent one. No halfway measures were taken. William Kent, the architect, started the trend early in the eighteen-hundreds when he designed gardens on the general principle: "Nature abhors a straight line." Then Sir William Chambers, who had lived in China for several years, in 1750 planned the first Chinese garden in England. In it he laid out curves instead of straight lines, making use of the natural features of the land. He favored unclipped trees introduced for accent, rather than clipped trees used for geometric pattern. By the time Lancelot Brown, usually referred to as Capability Brown, was appointed Royal Gardener at Hampton Court and Kew Gardens, the trend only needed undeviating direction, which it certainly attained at the hands of the fashionable Capability. Hardly a garden he touched retained anything of its earlier characteristics. Great open lawns rolled right up to house foundations, and winding walks through groves and woods suddenly revealed vistas which included ruins, temples and grottoes. Artificial lakes, such as the one at Blenheim Palace, were made, and the flower garden practically disappeared. What was left of it was relegated to a well hidden area which contained the fruit and kitchen garden as well. Those who loved plants turned to raising and forcing them in conservatories and hothouses. There was a scientific interest in horticulture and botany, but real floral beauty in the garden was not to be recaptured until the early years of the nineteenth century.

This explains why the artists, following the style of the day, for the most part placed their sitters in outdoor backgrounds. Flowers in the hair, at the throat, or carried in baskets reveal the love for flowers, but it is only in the occasional "conversation piece" painting, such as Hogarth's denunciation of gambling in *The Lady's Last Stake* (Fig. 90),

Figure 96. "Queen Charlotte," by John Zoffany. Delphinium and roses are a beautiful combination for either royal palace or humble home.

that we see the homey touch of flowers used in room decoration. The large bouquets placed in fireplaces can also be found on occasion in these more informal paintings (Fig. 91), but even the social satirists such as Rowlandson omit them as distracting. There are exceptions, of course, and we find Allan Ramsay suggesting a large arrangement of flowers in his portrait of his wife (Fig. 94), and Zoffany included a fine vase massed with flowers in several paintings of the royal family of George III (Figs. 95 and 96). Benjamin West, possibly because of his American heritage, did not include a typically British mass bouquet in his portrait of Mrs. Thomas Wyld of Sheen (Fig. 97), but painted only a group of roses placed in a vase that might have been oriental in origin. Robert Sayer's charming bouquets, engraved in his *New Book of Flowers* in 1779, might well be copied today with living flowers, their designing is so attractive (Fig. 98).

It is disappointing indeed not to find many genuine examples of what we call Georgian flower arrangements, for we know they existed, and it is tantalizing not to have original models. Within the many real and pseudo-Georgian rooms in American interiors today, massed groups of beautiful garden and fine hothouse flowers certainly have a place. The best we can do, if we want to create a feeling of the eighteenth century, is to treat them naturally and gracefully and place them in appropriate vases, either antique or authentic copies. If we feel obliged to be literal (as can well happen in a flower show), we should include only those varieties of flowers which we know were grown in England during the Georgian period.

Figure 97. "Diana, Wife of Thomas Wyld of Sheen" (detail). Painted by the American-born English artist, Benjamin West, in 1766.

Above: Figure 98. Page from Robert Sayer's "A New Book of Flowers." Here is a chance to study effective ways of gaining depth when handling real flowers. In these designs flowers are turned to the side and to the back so that the eye is led around the arrangements. The one at the left is especially lovely.

Two early XIXth-century English flower vases. Above: Figure 99. Jardinière with cover. Silver resist lustre decoration on glazed earthenware. Left: Figure 100. Silver lustre.

Figure 101. Portrait of Elizabeth Paddy Wensley by an unknown artist. 1670-1680.

COLONIAL AND EIGHTEENTH-CENTURY AMERICA

WE AMERICANS have a deep and affectionate feeling for all the furniture and other objects we have inherited from our ancestors. Many a home in our country is today furnished with heirlooms of the past, either entirely or in combination with newer, more modern furnishings. To add the warmth and beauty of flowers to such a setting is a natural gesture. Needless to say, there are many kinds of receptacles which have both a natural affinity for the beauty of flowers and an appropriateness to the setting.

We must piece evidence together, however, if we wish to use our flowers in a manner similar to that in which they were enjoyed indoors in America several hundred years ago. There are too few American pictures in existence to reveal accurately and completely how flowers were used or "arranged" in those days, and there is little descriptive material in the old writings. We do know, however, what the flowers of colonial times were, from correspondence of the period, newspaper advertisements, and old account books and diaries. From these same sources we also know that vases were imported in the eighteenth century; but, lacking descriptions or pictorial representations, we can only assume that the arrangements were either informal bouquets or the display of a few choice blooms.

Colonial America of the seventeenth century seems to have developed three main cultural centers. In New England, where the first settlers came as religious dissenters, the harsh climate and rigorous living conditions left little leisure for the niceties of life.

Having cut themselves off from the mother country, the Pilgrims, the Puritans, and those who came later had to spend all their energy and time providing a living for their families. Gardens yielded food and medicine, and incidentally cosmetics and dyes. What flowers there were doubtless were grown as useful herbs, within small dooryard gardens similar to those the settlers had left behind in England. The peony had been known from ancient times for its healing properties; from rose petals a syrup for sore throats, a pain soother, and a purge could be made; marigolds added to hot drinks provided a stimulant and could induce perspiration for the reduction of fever; and hollyhocks were used for voiding "stones and gravel." All these must have been brought over by the settlers. These intrepid people brought seeds, cuttings, and bulbs of many other flowers, carefully treasured, on the long voyage across the Atlantic. The plants which sprang from them were depended upon not only to flavor food and repel clothes moths and fleas, but to succor teething babies, relieve earaches, headaches and sore muscles, ease childbirth, induce sleep, serve as mild cathartics, heal wounds, and serve as poultices.

The lovely New England countryside had many native wild flowers, such as black-eyed Susan, goldenrod and asters, and many flowering trees and shrubs, such as dogwood, laurel, shadbush, and sumac, to name but a few. These provided readily obtainable flowering material, although in the early days there was constant danger from the Indians, and little leisure for a walk in any case.

An English traveler, John Josselyn, who had made two trips to New England, in 1638 and 1663, wrote a little book called *New England Rarities Discovered* in which he mentioned that certain English herbs prospered in the new world. Among them were: "marygolds, French mallowes, gillyflowers, and roses." His account of his second voyage tells us that by then the settlers had succeeded in introducing fruit trees; and apples, pears, quinces, cherries, and plums all flourished.

The Pilgrim Society of Plymouth, Massachusetts, owns one of the earliest American portraits known, one which is of special interest to us because it includes flowers (Fig.101). In it Elizabeth Paddy Wensley, a lady of character and sensitivity, looks out from beneath her kerchief with a steady eye. Her portrait tells us that, by the time of the 1670's, life in the Plymouth colony had eased enough for her to put on her best dress to be painted by the unknown artist who has recorded her for history, along with the few flowers we suppose were from her own garden. They include roses, tulips, a bicolor carnation, and an unidentified six-petaled flower. The glass vase that holds her flowers was probably a prized possession brought from abroad.

Nieuw Amsterdam, which was settled in 1626, grew and flourished as a little center of Dutch culture in the New World until taken over by the English in 1664. Following the horticultural practices of Holland, the Dutch settlers were soon known for the excellence of their orchards. In his *Description of The New Netherlands*, Adriaen Van der Donck, writing in 1655, said these included apple, pear, peach, plum, and cherry trees. He found that the lilac had been introduced and in the old Dutch manner called it the "clove tree"—its every tiny floret resembling a clove. Among garden flowers, he mentioned "white and red roses of different kinds," which included the briar rose or eglantine, hollyhock (called stock rose because of its tall, straight stalk), and peony (called St. Cornelis rose). Several kinds of carnations, gillyflowers (these included pinks, stocks, Sweet William, and rocket), "different varieties of fine tulips, white lilies, the lily fruitularia [crown imperial], anemones, baredames, violets, and marigolds" (calendula), were also among the cultivated flowers he saw. "Baredames" is the *Colchicum*, or autumn crocus, which flowers on a bare stalk in the fall, its leaves having appeared and died down in the spring. The flowers are either purple or white and in the old writings are frequently referred to as "naked ladies, baredames, or naked boys." Of the native plants he described, we recognize the wild sunflower, our red wood lily, and the yellow *Lilium canadense*.

The Dutch of Nieuw Amsterdam perhaps had a little more time to enjoy their flowers

Figure 102. Linen coverlet (detail) made in New York around 1800. The natural attraction of a profuse bouquet is beautifully realized.

than their compatriots farther up the Hudson River or the Massachusetts Bay colonists, for life was safer for them. If flowers "decked" their rooms, they would likely have been placed in stoneware jugs, simple pottery utensils, or pewter containers, for such articles were doubtless brought over from Holland.

While the northern settlements were constantly bracing themselves against the elements or their unfriendly neighbors, those in Virginia were also often in a state of turmoil because of danger from Indians and also because of troubles at home in England. The Virginia colonists had remained affiliated with the Church of England and were never really separated from the mother country. Consequently they were more affected by the upheavals of the century in England, the Civil War of James the First's reign, Oliver Cromwell's Commonwealth, and Charles the Second's Restoration, as well as the bloodless revolution which brought William and Mary to the throne in 1689. However, by 1698, when Williamsburg was founded as the capital city, the life of the colony had taken on a far more gracious aspect than that of New England, for a favorable balance of trade, together with slave labor, was bringing wealth and leisure to the people. Tobacco, rice, indigo, and cotton were all grown on a large scale and sent abroad. In turn fine furniture, textiles, wallpapers, and chinaware were imported in ever increasing quantity as the eighteenth century progressed; and flowering plants, shrubs, and fruit trees traveled the ocean in both directions. Each American planter had an agent in London who managed his affairs there, made the required purchases of furniture, china, plants and so forth, and arranged their transportation to the colony.

One of our best sources of information about the plant materials that were exchanged between the colonies and England is the correspondence between John Bartram of Philadelphia and Peter Collinson of London. Collinson was a wealthy wool merchant who was

Opposite page: Figure 103. Portrait of Eleanor Darnall by Justus Englehardt Kuhn. The artist, a German, worked in the vicinity of Annapolis between 1708 and 1717. While the details of this scene—the garden and the great urn with its mask—are strictly European, the bouquet has a New World flavor, for the tulips, roses, and pinks shown in the urn were all well established in American gardens by this time.

Figure 104. A Stiegel-type tumbler, in any of its different-size variations, would have made a useful and beautiful flower container in the eighteenth century. Copley suggests such a use in this portrait of Mrs. Blackstone.

Figure 105. Portrait of Mrs. Benjamin Blackstone by John Singleton Copley. The glass tumbler, very possibly a flip glass, holds pink, blue, and white flowers.

passionately devoted to horticultural interests as a hobby. Bartram was a dedicated naturalist who traveled up and down the length of the eastern seaboard exploring new regions and discovering new plants. One of the first to make use of the system of binominal nomenclature propounded by Linnaeus[1] in 1735, he not only recorded the native plants but studied the animals, birds, insects, and molluscs of the territory through which he traveled. Employed by Collinson, Philip Miller, and certain members of the aristocracy, he was responsible for the introduction into England of over one hundred and fifty species of our native trees, shrubs, and wild flowers. To his own botanical garden, on the banks of the Schulkyll river at Kingessing, came a variety of flowering material sent to him by his enthusiastic supporters on the other side of the Atlantic. This was sent in the form of bulbs, seeds, and seedlings, and the patience of all parties concerned in effecting these exchanges is almost beyond belief. In reading their letters, we learn of many failures and

---

[1] Carolus Linnaeus, the Swedish botanist (1707–1778), established binominal nomenclature (genera and species) of botany and zoology. He published *Systema Naturae*, 1735, and *Species Plantarum*, 1753.

Opposite: Figure 106. Mary Brewton Alston of Charleston, South Carolina, painted in 1798 by Edward Savage. The bouquet of flowers in the glass vase includes foxgloves, pinks, and roses. Delicately painted, they add a gay touch to this portrait of a charming lady.

Several types of ceramic vases frequently imported by the American colonies during the eighteenth century are represented on these pages. Below: Figure 107. Dutch Delft vase. Late XVIIth or early XVIIIth century. Tin-enameled earthenware with blue and white decoration.

Above: Figure 108. Chinese export porcelain bowl of a type often referred to as Lowestoft (1736-1795). Great quantities of this ware, including bowls of many sizes and flower holders with perforated tops, reached America.

Right: Figure 109. Portrait of Mrs. George Watson by John Singleton Copley (1738-1815). Into the great port of Boston in the pre-Revolutionary period came many luxuries from abroad. This colonial lady holds in her hand a blue and white "china" vase containing a parrot tulip and two checkered lilies (Fritillaria meleagris) which undoubtedly grew from "roots" imported from Holland.

Above, left: Figure 110. Pennsylvania-German flower holder of glazed earthenware with slip decoration. One of the few ceramic wares made in America before the nineteenth century. Above, right: Figure 111. XVIIIth-century Bristol pottery, blue and white "brick." This was meant either for flowers or for ink and quills.

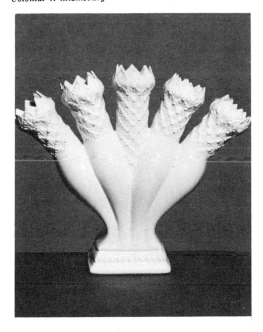

Above: Figure 112. Five-fingered posy holder. English cream ware, XVIIIth century.

Figure 113. Needlepoint fire screen worked by Nellie Custis. Spring flowers in a blue container with white overlay, possibly copied from a Wedgwood vase.

disappointments which were due to careless ship captains, who sometimes let the consignments be doused with salt spray, allowed them to dry out for lack of water, or let them rot because of too much water.

In 1737, Bartram wrote that lilacs were thriving in the colonies. The following year he wrote of tulips, "We have a great variety obtained from the breeders which we have had these many years." From Collinson, on Oct. 20, 1740, came this letter: "Dear Friend, inclosed is the Mate's receipt for a box of bulbs, directed for thee. Make much of them; for they are such a collection as is rarely to be met with, all at once: for all the sorts of bulbous roots being taken up this year, there is some of every sort. There is above 20 sorts of Crocus—as many of Narcissus—all our sorts of Martagons and Lilies—with Gladiolus, Ornithogalums, Moleys (*Allium Moly*), and Irises, with many others I don't now remember, which time will show thee. It is likely some sorts thee may have; but I believe there is more that you have not. So pray take great care of them. Give them a good soil, and keep them clear from weeds, which are a great prejudice to these flowers in the spring."

Elsewhere in their correspondence we learn that Bartram received tuberoses, fraxinella, the double yellow rose, a moss rose, china aster, and carnations, of which he wrote in 1761: "I have now a glorious appearance of carnations from thy seed—the brightest colors that ever eyes beheld."

As Bartram indicated when he wrote of tulips, it was not unusual for the colonists to import bulbs from Holland, and a number of newspaper advertisements during the eighteenth century announced the arrival of "roots" which included, besides tulips, hyacinths and daffodils. Even "flower root glasses" (hyacinth vases) were advertised for sale. The lovely red and purple *"Ranunculus anemones"* which once again bloom in the gardens of Williamsburg were also included in the listing of these "roots."

Dried flowers were quite commonly gathered and bunched for the winter months. Native materials which we definitely know to have been used included pearly everlasting, sea lavender, and bittersweet; sumac, alder, and cattails, as well as other berries and seed pods, could also have been used. Gardens contributed globe amaranth, honesty, and straw flowers, which Philip Miller tells us were placed in vases filled with sand.

During these busy years there had been no time for the American colonists to experiment with native clays to any great extent, nor with chemicals for glazing, so the arts of the potter had made little progress during two centuries. Lacking encouragement to do so, ceramic craftsmen had not immigrated to these shores. Pewter manufacture, silversmithing, and glassmaking were practised, and provided the people with necessary utensils. It was left to the English to export the lovely ceramic wares which helped to satisfy the craving for just a little luxury and extravagance, and at last colonial women had real vases to use for their flowers. There were five-fingered "posey holders," conventional vase shapes, and many holders with spouts or perforated tops, the same as used in England.

Naturally enough, Chinese wares which were sought after by the Europeans found their way to America as well. By the last quarter of the eighteenth century, dinnerware was being ordered in sets, and bowls of all sizes, pitchers, jars, and flower holders were arriving here in quantity. Collinson, an ever useful and delightful source of information, wrote of placing dried globe amaranths in "flower potts and China basons." Lowestoft bowls filled with sand would certainly have done the trick. Many families ordered sets of five decorative vases which followed the lines of fine Chinese porcelains and were sold as garnitures for the mantelpiece.

With abundant flowering material, both native and cultivated, with a little more time to pursue the more leisurely household duties, and with containers at hand, it is certain that many a housewife took joy in arranging bouquets to brighten her home. Fresh flowers in spring and summer, dried flowers and berries in winter, all served to brighten the parlors of colonial America.

AN ARTICLE in *Godey's Lady's Book* for January, 1855, begins: "Of all modes of enlivening the aspect of an apartment, there is perhaps none more pleasing than the sight of plants and flowers suitably arranged and distributed. They are ornaments of Nature's own producing, which inspire an interest apart from their beauty, by the care and attention required for their culture. They employ the hand, delight the eye, and inform and edify the mind, and, unlike many artificial objects, the enjoyment and instruction they afford are within the reach of all, the poor may partake as well as the rich."

Never a month went by without this eagerly-awaited magazine telling its subscribers how to care for flowers, what flowers to grow, or how to make bits of fancywork to adorn their vases of cut flowers. There is good common sense in much of what contributors wrote about arranging flowers and much of horticultural interest in the listings and descriptions of available or new plant materials, as well as many suggestions which reflect a tasteless and sentimental era.

By the time Queen Victoria ascended the throne, in 1837, flower horizons had broadened to such an extent that much of the flowering material we have today was in cultivation. During the previous century, all the many native European plants and bulbs known for so long in English gardens had reached America from England. Now South African flowers such as the gladiolus, Mexican dahlias and nasturtiums, azaleas, camellias, tree peonies, and new varieties of chrysanthemums and roses from China took their places in American gardens.

The African gladiolus, introduced about 1830, soon became popular with hybridizers because of its rich and varied colors. Within thirty years these were described as "yellow, red, scarlet and white, shaded rose, orange, delicate pink, bright scarlet shaded with orange, and yellow." The dahlia had also become a highly esteemed flower, and one tempting to the hybridizers; so much so that it was noticed that the dahlia and the pansy had replaced the auricula and tulip in the affections of the florists, an affection which had held sway for two hundred years. The fuchsia, otherwise known as "ladies ear drops," also achieved great popularity after its introduction and is very frequently seen in Currier and Ives flower prints and in water-color paintings. Henderson made great strides in improving the zinnia, nurserymen were importing and improving many kinds of lilies, and the appeal of the beauty and good keeping qualities of chrysanthemums grew rapidly. Although pink hues were not developed at the time, there was great variety achieved in the variations of yellow, brown, and red. The November, 1856, issue of *Godey's* magazine mentioned the Chinese chrysanthemum as having been introduced a hundred years previously, but reported that there were innumerable varieties and sub-varieties of recent introduction.

Bleeding-heart, also from China, was described as of recent introduction in 1858, and was called "one of the most striking objects in the whole range of floral attractions."

Among the old European flowers, much improvement had been made. Snapdragons were so developed that by mid-century a London author wrote that they were "now of a color deep as the crimsoned purple tide which flows in living veins—now of a pale and soft rose colored hue—or sometimes of a white tint shaded with a faint blush of pink." *Godey's* informed its readers that there were "new, large flowering varieties of German ten week stock which were superb," and that the improvement made in the Pansy, or Heart's-ease, within a few years would surprise those to whom it was not familiar. "From the ordinary Johnny-jump-up, scarcely the size of a sixpence," the magazine went on to say, "our friend Dreer (Henry A. Dreer, Philadelphia) has produced varieties so large that they could not be covered with a Spanish dollar, and they are of the most exquisite colors."

The entire nineteenth century was a period of great enthusiasm for flowers, plants, and gardening. The invention of the Wardian case (what we would now call a terrarium) started a craze for indoor gardening. Bay windows burgeoned with house plants, and conservatories were added to houses so that newly discovered exotics could be grown. These usually included a number of ornamental foliage plants such as agaves, crotons, caladiums, dracaenas, ferns, marantas, and rubber plants. People became avid collectors of certain plants, specializing in such popular flowers as begonias, geraniums, fuchsias, and camellias.

Because fashionable English gardens were laid out in beds of solid color provided by compact and low growing plants, it was suggested that a cutting garden be set apart to supply the flowers for cutting. "Were this to be done in all gardens where cut flowers

Figure 114. Portrait of Mary and Emily McEuen, painted by Thomas Sully in 1823. (Detail.) The sketchbook held by one of the young ladies is entitled "Sketches from Nature," and in all likelihood she was about to paint on one of its pages the lovely bouquet in the green glass vase.

Figure 115. "The Children of Israel and Sarah Ann Griffith," painted by Oliver Tarbell Eddy about 1844. (Detail.) The compactness of the bouquets and the nosegay, their outlines softened by delicate green foliage, are quite typically Victorian.

are in request," said the *Floral World and Garden Guide* (a magazine), "much vexation between the gardener and his employers would be avoided; the employer would be saved the annoyance of not having sufficient, and the gardener the vexation of having the flowers stripped off plants in beds occupying prominent positions." In America, though round beds of cannas and geraniums dotted the lawns of well-kept places, the problem was not so acute, for backyards always sheltered the flowering shrubs and rose bushes, as well as the beds of perennials and annuals, which were there to be picked and to be enjoyed indoors.

A properly educated young lady of the Victorian era was able to portray all these lovely garden flowers in water color, and if she could not do it in freehand, there were copybooks for her use. (Fig. 114.) She learned how to make wax and feather flowers, which were placed under glass domes, and to compose floral designs made of leather, seeds, and hair.

Another desirable accomplishment was that of fashioning nosegays, for no well-dressed lady ever appeared at a social gathering without one. A nosegay was often made at home, but might be received from an admirer, in which case its composition was significant, for sentimental meanings were attached to various flowers, and a message could be sent by combining certain ones. The "language of flowers" was carefully studied, and many a courtship made progress through the sending and receiving of nosegays. Sweet-scented flowers were naturally chosen. Mignonette, roses, lilies-of-the-valley, sweet peas, violets, bouvardia, carnations, and pinks, all contributed their delicious scents. The importance attached to the nosegay is apparent when we read in *Godey's* for May, 1855, "To get a half dozen of mixed flowers bundled together anyhow, and go into good company with such a nosegay in these days, is looked upon as certainly not a mark of high breeding."

With this genuine as well as sentimental interest in flowers was coupled a desire to

95

display them in vases, on the center tables of Victorian parlors, on mantelpieces, and on dining-room tables. Writing in 1838, Edward Sayers in his *American Flower Garden Companion* noted that it was "now an almost universal practice to have cut flowers in rooms as natural ornaments." Therefore, he added, "Some hints relative to the management of them may perhaps be of service to their fair patrons." What he suggested were the same principles for caring for flowers that we follow today, and which the Italian author Ferrari treated in the 17th century. Sayers' rules were first, to change the water frequently and second, to cut off half an inch or an inch of stem to open up pores that had become "closed with glutinous matter that had exuded from the stem when first cut."

That the Mid-Victorians liked brilliant-hued flowers and used strong color contrasts in their grouping is evidenced by the following suggestions for arranging a bouquet, taken from *Godey's.* "There is no doubt that arranging flowers according to their contrast or complementary colors, is more pleasing to the eye than placing them according to their harmonies," says the writer. "Consequently a blue flower should be placed next an orange flower, a yellow near a violet, and a red or white should have plants with abundant foliage near them." In an era of red plush and black horsehair, and of gardens "bedded out" with blue lobelia, red geraniums, and yellow-green coleus foliage, it is small wonder that such bouquets were preferred. Another author suggested combinations a little less startling, such as "rose color and pale blue, white, lilac, mauve or purple with primrose, dark blue and brilliant scarlet, cerise or cherry with white, blue, white and rose." These ideas were set forth in a book called *Window Gardening,* and subtitled *Devoted Specially to the Culture of Flowers and Ornamental Plants for Indoor Use and Parlor Decoration.* The author warned against allowing "little dabs of white" to be scattered all over an assortment of flowers, preferring to see the white used as an outer edging. To emphasize ways to get the best effects from flower-filled vases, he neatly tied up the idea with the craze for "fancy-work" as follows: "In arranging flowers it is well to bear in mind the laws of worsted work, and when we desire to adorn our rooms with flowers we should consider the grounding to be prepared for them, as if it were a cushion." This means, we suppose, simply that they should have a proper background.

Many different suggestions and opinions were voiced by various authors on the subject of color and the arranging of flowers. Perhaps the one point they did agree on, however, was the initial assumption that a great many flowers would be grouped in any bouquet. Books and magazine articles all extolled the beauty of flowers and were in agreement that the art of arranging them was an accomplishment all ladies should acquire. Young girls of the 1870's were able to learn from the *St. Nicholas Magazine* just how to manage flowers; I quote at length from a typically Victorian article from that magazine. "Many persons who are lucky enough to have flowers do not at all know how to arrange them so as to produce the best effect, while others seem born with a knack for doing such things in just the right way. Knack cannot be taught, but there are a few rules and principles on the subject so simple that even a child can understand and follow them and if you St. Nicholas girls will keep them in mind when you have flowers to arrange, I think you will find them helpful. Just as flowers are the most beautiful decoration which any house can have, so the proper management of them is one of the gracefullest of arts, and everything which makes home prettier and more attractive is worth study and pains, so I will tell you what these rules are in the hope that you will use and apply them yourselves.

"1st. The *color* of the vase to be used is of importance. Gaudy reds and blues should never be chosen, for they conflict with the delicate hues of the flowers. Bronze or black vases, dark green, pure white, or silver, always produce a good effect, and so does a straw basket, while clear glass, which shows the graceful clasping of the stems, is perhaps prettiest of all.

"2nd. The shape of the vase is also to be thought of. For the middle of a dinner-table, a round bowl is always appropriate, or a tall vase with a saucer-shaped base. Or, if the

Figure 116. "Fruit and Flowers." Painting by unknown American artist made about 1835.

center of the table is otherwise occupied, a large conch shell, or shell-shaped dish, may be swung from the chandelier above, and with plenty of vines and feathering green, made to look very pretty. Delicate flowers, such as lilies-of-the-valley and sweet-peas, should be placed by themselves in slender tapering glasses; violets should nestle their fragrant purple in some tiny cup, and pansies be set in groups, with no gayer flowers to contradict their soft velvet hues; and—this is a hint for summer—few things are prettier than balsam blossoms, or double variegated hollyhocks, massed on a flat plate, with a fringe of green to hide the edge. No leaves should be interspersed with these; the plate will look like a solid mosaic of splendid color.

"3rd. *Stiffness* and crowding are the two things to be specially avoided in arranging flowers. What can be uglier than the great tasteless bunches into which the ordinary florist ties his wares, or what more extravagant. A skillful person will untie one of these, and, adding green leaves, make the same flowers into half a dozen bouquets, each more effective than the original. Flowers should be grouped as they grow, with a cloud of light foliage in and about them to set off their forms and colors. Don't forget this.

"4th. It is better, as a general rule, not to put more than one or two sorts of flowers into the same vase. A great bush with roses, and camellias, and carnations, and feverfew, and geraniums growing on it all at once would be a frightful thing to behold; just so a monstrous bouquet made up of all these flowers is meaningless and ugly. Certain flowers, such as heliotrope, mignonette, and myrtle, mix well with everything; but usually it is

97

Above: Figure 117. "The York Family at Home," 1837. The flowers are arranged in a type of vase which is frequently reproduced in iron today.

Left: Figure 118. Pennsylvania-German birth certificate, 1852.

98

Right: Figure 119. Two brilliantly colored vases of pressed Sandwich glass (1835-1865).

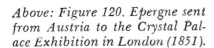

Above: Figure 120. Epergne sent from Austria to the Crystal Palace Exhibition in London (1851).

Opposite, left: Figure 121. Vase for preserving flowers. "Godey's Lady's Book," August 1858, states: "Take a vase and fill it with flowers, arranged to suit the taste, and of as many varieties as the person pleases, carefully sealing the stem of each flower (with sealing or beeswax) before placing it in the vase. Place the vase upon a wooden stand, and place the shade over it. Be careful that flowers, vase and shade are perfectly dry. Fill up groove in the wood, in which the shade stands with melted wax. By covering it with chenille, it can be perfectly hidden."

Right: Figure 122. "Elizabeth," one of the popular "name" lithographs of the Victorian era.

Vases shown in the catalogue of the Exhibition of the Industry of All Nations, New York, 1853-1854.

Extreme left: Figure 123. Bohemian glass vases manufactured by E. Stainer. Left: Figure 124. An elaborate vase from Messrs. Haviland, Brothers and Co., Limoges.

better to group flowers with their kind—roses in one glass, geraniums in another, and not try to make them agree in companies.

"5th. When you do mix flowers, be careful not to put colors which clash side by side. Scarlets and pinks spoil each other; so do blues and purples, and yellows and mauves. If your vase or dish is a very large one, to hold a great number of flowers, it is a good plan to divide it into thirds or quarters, making each division perfectly harmonious within itself, and then blend the whole with lines of green and white, and soft neutral tint. Every group of mixed flowers requires one little touch of yellow to make it vivid; but this must be skillfully applied. It is good practice to experiment with this effect. For instance, arrange a group of maroon, scarlet, and white geraniums with green leaves, and add a single blossom of gold-colored calceolaria, and you will see at once that the whole bouquet seems to flash out and become more brilliant.

"Lastly. Love your flowers. By some subtle sense the dear things always detect their friends, and for them they will live longer and bloom more freely than they ever will for a stranger. And I can tell you, girls, the sympathy of a flower is worth winning, as you will find out when you grow older, and realize that there are such things as dull days which need cheering and comforting."

There is a great deal of sound advice here (though I think few would find a conch shell swinging from the chandelier quite in keeping with present-day decorating ideas!) Here once again there are definite ideas about color combinations, and one suspects that even in Victorian times there was nothing more personal than color preferences. The article also shows that a reaction was setting in against the padded contours of earlier Victorian bouquets. The period was now that of the 1870's, and a more naturalistic approach to beauty was beginning to be felt.

Aside from the massing of gay colors, we know the Victorians loved to include foliage and grasses in their bouquets. "Green is essential in all bouquets, and the foliage of the respective flowers is always best fitted to show off their peculiar charms," wrote the author of *Window Gardening*. The passage continued, "Nevertheless a feathery and plumey green adds grace to all arrangements of flowers, and variegated foliage is exceedingly pretty for bordering bouquets, baskets and flat dishes." Begonia leaves and those of *Cissus discolor* were much used for this purpose, and ivy and maiden hair fern were also desirable. It was thought that "The leaves of the scarlet geranium preserve many flowers by their velvety texture which retains so much moisture"; and it was therefore recommended that a leaf or two be included in any group of cut flowers. Striped ribbon grass is often seen in old flower prints, and feathery grasses and dock seem often to have been included in bunches of flowers. In fact, it became very fashionable to bring Nature indoors, as *Godey's* tells us, by gathering "the various grasses of the season and allowing them to dry in a dark room before tastefully arranging them in a vase or pretty basket. Wheat, oats, and rye, as well as the various tall grasses to be found everyplace in the country, make beautiful ornaments for the parlor."

Indeed, nature appreciation was part of the Victorian character, as well as the inclination to do a bit of preaching or moralizing. "It has long been a matter of surprise," remarks one writer, "to observe how very seldom we find any use made of the actual products of our woods and fields, of things which may be found occupying the earth or air of our own country, or even the deep seas that surround our shores, in ornamenting our houses. We do sometimes find cases of stuffed birds, or animals, or preserved butterflies and beetles, and more frequently a little stand of geraniums. Even flowers are neglected. Go into the houses of twenty of the most elegant and educated people who live near you, and in how many will you find flowers upon their tables? They will show you their conservatories and greenhouses full of gorgeous blossoms, but you will find none brightening the dull marble slabs in the drawing-room, or, if you do, they will be the clumsily-arranged bunches which the servants have received from the gardener, and placed there without any attention to the graces of form and harmony of coloring. There are exceptions, happily; for in some houses you see artistic and ever-varying arrangements of these most lovely ornaments, and perceive at once that the eye and hand that have placed them within their crystal houses have been those of one who looked on them with love, whose taste would have been offended had one blossom stood out of the exact place where it most truly blended or contrasted with that next it, or its form had not exactly filled the very spot best fitted for it. You will see also that a taste and a judgment have been exercised in suiting the vase to the flowers, or the flowers to the vase, so that each group may be so perfect in itself that a painter would long to perpetuate it by his art. But this talent for flower decoration is rare; and we are disposed to think that it is too much confined to one class of people, those who occupy the middle rank in life, and, having

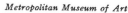

Figure 125. Not until the nineteenth century did it become customary to place flowers upon the dining table. This watercolor, painted in 1826, shows the Emperor of Austria's table. Appropriately the crown imperial (Fritillaria imperialis) takes its place at the top of the bouquet.

had but little wealth wherewith to procure purchased luxuries, and but few servants at their command, have been in a manner forced to gratify that taste for ornament which seems to be inherent in the human mind, by seeking its supplies from the fields of nature."

Antique shops today are filled with yesterday's Victorian vases. Because the desire for flowers was coupled with a craze for bric-a-brac, parlors blossomed forth with pairs of ornate mantel vases, with glass domes protecting real or artificial flowers, and with porcelains brought home by clipper ship from China. Flowers were placed in a variety of vases. Of these, many were imported, but many were of domestic manufacture. Some were purely ornamental and others were really useful. Perhaps the most versatile material was glass. There was milk glass, colorful moulded glass, satin glass, and pressed glass. From Austria and Bohemia came overlay glass, ruby-red glass with etched designs, and light-colored, opaque glass with gold decorations. England manufactured Bristol glass, a ware with a sanded finish and painted designs, and France made fragile and slender vases with flaring rims, often mounting the pieces in ormolu.

The very elaborate porcelain vases with hand-painted decorations and applied modeling which seem to typify the entire Victorian period were turned out by the hundreds of pairs, at both the Sèvres and the Haviland factory at Limoges. In the United States, at Bennington, Vermont, the unusual and much sought-after Parian ware was manufactured from a very fine white clay. This was left in its biscuit state, unglazed, but ornamented with modeled grapes, leaves, tendrils, and festoons.

Purely ornamental were the alabaster pieces beloved by the flower arranger today; and the elaborate metal ewers, supposedly copied from Benevenuto Cellini's work, belong in the same category. Both of these added the note of "elegance" to a room which the Victorian homemaker deemed important.

Humbler objects for holding flowers were fashioned by women who were clever with their hands and who never allowed themselves to be without some kind of "fancywork." The same ladies who crocheted antimacassars and made carpet slippers of Berlin wools also concocted fascinatingly awful mats to place under vases, and actually turned glass pickle-jars into vases by disguising them with wired worsted work. Plain glass vases were turned into a semblance of porcelain by a process known as potichomanie, a "beautiful and ladylike amusement," according to Peterson's Magazine. This technique employed pictures of flowers, birds, Chinese figurines, and other subjects, which were pasted inside a glass vase. A coat of varnish was next applied, and then paint was rolled around inside. The outside thus became quite colorful, since the designs showed through, and gold sometimes banded the rim. As the last step, several coats of varnish were applied to the exterior.

Baskets and epergnes round out the list of flower containers. Godey's book advised that the baskets be filled with wet sand and covered with sprigs of green, such as myrtle, arborvitae, or geranium leaves, before cut flowers were stuck in. A similar idea for the handling of épergnes was advanced by an English writer who recommended that shallow trays of zinc be made to fit the different parts of the epergne. These were to be made in two pieces in order to fit around the central stem. The pans were to be filled with "sandy peat" into which would be dibbed pieces of dwarf-growing lycopodiums (club moss) or Selaginella denticulata. Nursed along in a greenhouse or conservatory, these were ever ready to provide a groundwork for flowers, leaves, and fruit whenever an occasion for their use arose.

Victorian taste seemed to grow progressively worse. The industrial revolution early in the century had thrown many artist-craftsmen out of work, and the appreciation and understanding of fine design was lost with them. In England, William Morris tried to arouse interest in the betterment of the decorative arts, but it was an uphill fight. By the seventies, when Charles Eastlake published his Hints on Household Taste, interior

THE FLOWER VASE.

Figure 126. An exceptionally beautiful Currier & Ives lithograph. The fuchsia, the double China asters, and the dahlia, all seen in this arrangement, were great favorites of the mid-Victorian period. The moss rose, an old-time garden flower, had been popular since the early days of the eighteenth century.

103

decoration had reached its lowest ebb. Nevertheless, with Morris leading the way, with Whistler pointing out "the superior qualities of Oriental blue and white ware" to tawdry European objects, and with the pre-Raphaelites re-examining the motivation of painting, change was in the air and artistic values were re-assessed.

Even flower arranging felt the change. The author of *The English Flower Garden*, W. Robinson, whose book remained a standard work on horticulture for many years, wrote in 1883 that in arranging flowers one should "seek unity, harmony and simplicity of effect, rather than complexities, many of which involve much wearisome labour." He desired to see ways used "distinctly apart from the old nosegay masses and the modern jumble," preferring arrangements of one kind of flower only, such as Fantin-Latour had painted (Fig. 129). Japanese ways with plant material which showed "the beauty of form and line in a single twig or branch" were not only appreciated but strongly recommended to the English people in view of their many spring flowering shrubs, and old Japanese bronzes were highly praised for holding flowers. Of vases, he wrote that they had "shared the fate of most manufactured things within the past generation—they suffer from the mania for overdoing with designs called 'decorative.'" Therefore, his readers were advised to seek out containers which were not originally intended for flowers, such as Devonshire cream jars and ginger pots.

By the very end of this era, which had brought so much change to people's lives, flower arranging was actually suffering from over-simplification. One dozen carnations and some asparagus fern, placed in a tall cut-glass vase, sum up the state which flower arrangement had now reached.

LANDSCAPE, FRUIT AND FLOWERS.

Opposite page, top: Figure 129. Still life painted by the French artist Henri Fantin-Latour in 1866. This shows the type of bouquet the English author Robinson considered preferable to the "old nosegay masses and the modern jumble."

Opposite page, bottom: Figure 130. A very colorful Currier & Ives print of the year 1862, showing tightly massed flowers in a Parian ware vase.

Right: Figure 131. Currier & Ives lithograph of the mid-Victorian period. The tightness of the bouquet, the graceful green foliage at its edges, the paper frill, and the glass vase are all typically Victorian.

Below: Figure 132. "Desserte," an early painting by Henri Matisse, shows the popular late-Victorian use of the epergne. The maid is seen arranging flowers in the vase, while fruit is massed in the lower section.

Collection: Mrs. John Slade

Collection: Mr. Edward G. Robinson

Figure 133. A Victorian type of arrangement by the author. A Limoges vase holds popular Victorian flowers such as fuchsia, cockscomb, and roses. The strong contrasts of yellow, red, and white are typical; but, because they lack subtlety, they are not favored by today's arrangers.

CHINA, MOTHER OF GARDENS

Figure 134. Tomb painting. IXth century.

Courtesy of Langdon Warner and Harvard University Press

CHINA HAS LONG been known as "The Flowery Kingdom." It was named the "Mother of Gardens" by the great plant explorer, E. H. Wilson. China is extremely rich in flora and spectacular scenery; and she has produced artists and philosophers capable of capturing the very essence of Nature's beauty. In the arts, we find incipient floral motifs by the first century A.D. and great development in their use with the spread of Buddhism, whose sacred lotus soon became inseparably bound up with all forms of art expression. When times were turbulent, inspiration came to the artists from more restless and war-like sources, but during such epochs as the peaceful and prosperous centuries of the Sung dynasty (960-1280 A.D.) and the later Ming (1368-1644) and Ch'ing (1644-1912) dynasties, creative expression in every type of art form was strongly influenced by plant life. Paintings, textiles, and ceramics all extol the beauty of flowers.

In the Chinese home, flowers in vases, and plants, bulbs, and dwarfed trees in pots, have been commonplace touches for centuries. Courtyard gardens have been a feature of Chinese architecture, and the flower vendors who supplied the potted plants for them, as well as cut blossoms for the home, have been important to the Chinese way of life. The love of flowers is further exemplified by the way they have taken their place on the religious altars of household and temple alike, by the written words of the poets, by the masterpieces of the painters, even by the way the women have worn them in their hair. Yet, abundant as flowering material has always been, inspired as the people have been by Nature, and perceptive and knowledgeable as they are concerning her ways, the Chinese have never used flowers with the luxuriant exuberance of the European, who, as we have seen, loved large, colorful bouquets.

To interpret Chinese flower arrangements as we see them illustrated so frequently, we must first of all have some insight into three things: first, the art of *contemplation* as practiced by the followers of Confucius; second, the underlying principle of the *preservation of life* as taught by Buddhism; and third, the floral *symbolism* which has developed as a folklore.

Confucius taught that real enjoyment consists in simplicity. He wrote of the distraction that comes from viewing too much beauty and of the serenity to be gained from savouring one thing at a time. To view something such as the shadow of a tree cast on water, and then to project oneself into all it stands for—the structure of the tree, its changes with the seasons, its strength or its grace—is to gain knowledge and experience contentment. A few flowers in a vase can conjure up the whole life-history of a plant, as well as display the beauty of perfect blooms. Only when strong Western influence is evident or when the motif of the flower-filled basket appears do we find large numbers of varied flowers in a Chinese flower arrangement.

*Figure 135. Details from a large fresco painting in the tombs at Kuang Shêng Ssu.
XIVth century. One vase contains a few lotus blossoms and their leaves; the other,
peonies.*

The preservation of all life is one of the precepts of Buddhism. In accordance with this doctrine, which also prohibits the taking of life, the Chinese Buddhists use cut flowers sparingly. In fact, the typical Chinese garden does not provide a quantity of flowers for cutting. It is actually a small-scale replica of a natural landscape scene, or series of scenes, complete with water, weather-worn rocks, trees, and shrubs. Flowering plants and shrubs are introduced at strategic points to further the naturalism. The whole idea differs radically from that of the European, who strove in his gardens to conquer nature, rather than to follow it. The Western garden developed into an artificial setting for entertainment and a place for the collection of cultivated flowers. The Chinese garden, on the other hand, was a retreat and a place for contemplation. Trees and flowers owned the places in which they grew, and visitors came to see them. Lotuses planted in the ponds revealed the miracle of the perfect flower emerging from the mud. There were many lessons to be learned within the Chinese garden.

Within the secluded, paved courtyards of the average Chinese home, flowering material was carefully nurtured to brighten the scene and to be appreciated. Growing plants such as chrysanthemums have been massed in raised beds or brought in pots by the professional gardeners as the seasons progressed so that their development might be studied and they might be admired at the height of their perfection. Indoors, potted plants, tiny but very ancient trees trimmed by the hands of connoisseurs, and bulbs forced into bloom out of season, such as the paper-white narcissus of the New Year (which begins in February), have delighted the eye and tested the skill of the home-owner almost more than cut flowers. The raising of flowers was largely left to professional growers or to the intellectual horticulturalist who specialized in one particular type of plant.

It is true, however, that blossoms in vases have been set upon the altars of China since the beginning of the T'ang dynasty (618-906 A.D.), by which time Buddhism was widely accepted. Early flower containers were always utilitarian, and at this period they

110

were probably bottles or ceremonial wine vessels. The ancient *Ku* or bronze beaker which in both Han and pre-Han times (1122 B.C.-220 A.D.) held the sacrificial wines, was a beautiful and useful shape for holding flowers and was eventually copied in porcelain by later potters. Flower vases existed as such by the eleventh and twelfth centuries; pieces from that period exist for which no other possible use is known, and references to them are made in writings of the period. Paintings of two vases of great interest, one highly decorative, the other classically simple, are shown here (Fig. 135). They date from the fourteenth century and are details from a large Buddhist wall painting.

The Taoists, as well as the Buddhists and the followers of Confucius, have contributed to the story of Chinese flowers. In fact, much of the symbolism with which plant material is imbued has come from this religion. Flower Goddesses, the patron saints of florists, were referred to as *Hua Hsien*. They are usually seen in works of art carrying baskets of flowers, and frequently a hoe. Lan Ts'ai Ho, one of the Eight Immortals, who were legendary beings who attained immortality by studying Nature's secrets, is always shown with a flower-filled basket (Fig. 152). The basket is a favorite art motif in itself, being one of the hundred antiquities which figure in Chinese art (Fig. 156).

Chinese folklore concerning flowers, which over the centuries has become varied and complex, is full of interest. All flowers, because of their fragile beauty, are feminine, and have been given women's names. The four seasons are usually denoted by the white-blossomed *plum* of winter, the *peony* of springtime, the *lotus* of summer, and the fall *chrysanthemum*. Through the years, these have provided unlimited inspiration to painters, embroiderers, and porcelain designers. There were alternate seasonal flowers also,

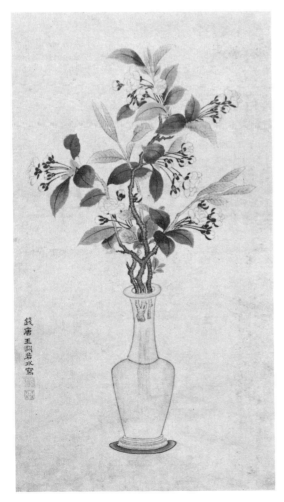

Left: Figure 137. Chun Yao vase. Sung dynasty (960-1279). Below: Figure 138. Early Ming or Yüan vase (1260-1368) decorated in blue underglaze.

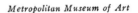

Metropolitan Museum of Art

Left: Figure 136. Peach blossoms in a glass vase. Painting in the style of a Yüan dynasty (1260-1368) painter.

Freer Gallery of Art, Washington

Left: Figure 139. Detail from a Ming dynasty (1368-1644) scroll painting. The single pine branch is so arresting that it gives almost the effect of an entire tree. The base for the vase reminds us that all the old Chinese vases were originally intended to be used with their own stands, one never being complete without the other. Unfortunately, through the centuries, most of these have become separated. Right: Figure 140. Herbaceous peonies in a decorative vase. XVIIIth-century painting on silk.

as the reader will notice when studying the tapestry scrolls reproduced here. Peach blossoms, for instance, are seen almost as frequently as those of the peony to symbolize spring. Certain combinations of plant material also were frequent, and we often see the "three friends of the cold season," pine, bamboo, and plum shown together.

The idea of longevity, or long life, greatly honored in China, was expressed by both the peach tree and the pear tree, by bamboo because of its great resiliency and durability, and by a certain fungus known as "the plant of long life." This fungus when picked hardens instead of shriveling, and its form is very frequently seen in various art mediums. The flower accorded the very highest honor was the tree peony *(Paeonia suffruticosa or P. Moutan).* This is often referred to as the "King of Flowers" and was symbolic of high position and wealth, as well as being an omen of good fortune. The narcissus which we know as the paper-white always had a New Year's association, as it was forced into bloom at that time to bring success, luck, and good fortune for the ensuing year. The orchid, the emblem of love and beauty, was also emblematic of fertility, as were the tiger lily and, of course, the pomegranate. Each month even had its own flower, but since varying flowers were chosen in different sections of the country, according to climatic conditions, lists given by various authors seldom agree.

Thus we find there are many things to be considered when we view a filled vase and try to understand the Chinese method of handling flowers. Symbolism, conservation of life, and the appreciation of beauty are all three inextricably bound up in what we see; perhaps we can best describe the Chinese use of flowers as restrained but never stylized. For further study it will not be amiss to go directly to the many finely painted delineations of blossoms, stems and leaves, in Chinese art. These are exquisite in their elimination of extraneous detail and in their simplification. Here we can really see the subtle working out of space relationships, the use of emphasis and unity, and the feeling for rhythm.

To list even a majority of the plants of China would fill a good sized botany. It is a vast country with great variation in climatic conditions. Since 1637, when the first English ships sailed there, many flowers, trees, and shrubs have found their way into our gardens directly from China and have become so ordinary to us that we no longer think of them as anything but commonplace. The Chinese, who seem to have had a flair for systematization, started to classify their plants at a very early date. Medicinal herbs and drugs were described accurately in the Han era (207 B.C.-220 A.D.), and as early as the eleventh century thirty-five varieties of chrysanthemums had already been recognized.

Figure 141. A large blue vase holds pine and flowering branches in this Ch'ing Dynasty painting. The dish at the left contains the fragrant citron, beloved by the Chinese and called "Buddha's hand."

Left: Figure 142. A tree peony, most revered of all flowers, is coupled with the early-flowering plum. The paper-white narcissus, symbolic of the New Year, and the fungus, symbolic of longevity, combine to make a meaningful picture. XVIIIth century. Above: Figure 143. Apple-green crackled-glaze vase. Below: Figure 144. Beaker-shaped vase, Clair de Lune glaze. Both K'ang Hsi period (1662-1722).

Figure 145. Yellow-glaze vase of the K'ang Hsi period (1662-1772).

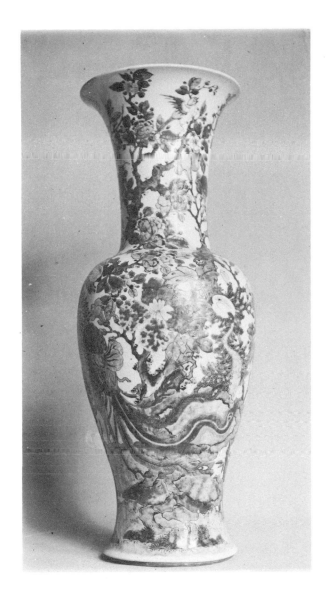

Left: Figure 146. Polychrome vase, famille verte, K'ang Hsi period.

Metropolitan Museum of Art

Figure 147. Peachbloom-glaze vase, K'ang Hsi period.

Four silk tapestry panels of the K'ang Hsi period (1662-1722), depicting the seasons. Above, left: Figure 148. Spring. Peach blossoms and an orchid spray, with peonies at the base of the vase. Above, right: Figure 149. Summer, with magnolia and tree peony. Right: Figure 150. Autumn, with osmanthus, a member of the olive family which is dearly loved by the Chinese because of its fragrance; chrysanthemums are at the base. Opposite (at left): Figure 151. Winter, with plum blossoms, bamboo, and berries. The paper-white narcissus of the New Year lies at the base. These panels are of interest not only because of the plant materials shown but also because of the vases, which were copied from ancient bronze forms.

Philadelphia Museum of Art

116

The list of the most familiar and popular native plant materials included at the end of this book has been made up from several sources. A seventeenth-century handbook for art students entitled *Chieh Tzu Yüan Hua Chuan*, which contains about seventy woodcuts of garden flowers and fruit blossoms, formed the basis of the list.

Below: Figure 152. Tapestry showing one of the Taoist immortals. On her shoulder rests a hoe on which is hung a basket of peonies. The flower basket is one of the hundred antiquities and is highly favored as a container. In her right hand the lady immortal holds the fungus that symbolizes long life, and the peach tree that symbolizes immortality is shown overhead.

Freer Gallery of Art, Washington

117

Left: Figure 154. Polychrome vase of the K'ang Hsi period (1662-1722). Famille noire. Below: Figure 155. Vase of the Chien Lung period (1736-1795). Famille rose.

Left: Figure 153. XIXth-century silk embroidery. Many interesting vase forms can be seen here, each on its own stand. The variety of plant material includes (from left to right) plum, pine, citron, lotus, orchid, magnolia, peony, peach, chrysanthemum, osmanthus, and narcissus Tazetta.

Right: Figure 156. The decoration of this porcelain jar features a basket filled with roses, peonies, yellow lilies, chrysanthemums, and lotus. Arrangements of massed flowers, such as this, are found in Chinese art only when they are displayed in such a basket or when direct Western influence is present.

Metropolitan Museum of Art

Metropolitan Museum of Art

120

Opposite page: Figure 157. Portrait of Mme. Wei I-chieh. In the beaker-shaped vase are narcissus and the fungus of long life. Right: Figure 158. Vase of the Chien Lung period (1736-1795). Turquoise-blue monochrome. Below: Figure 159. A Chinese gentleman seated with his Pekingese dog. At his elbow is a ceramic vase holding what seem to be hosta blossoms. From "The Pictorial News," illustrated by Wang Taon, 1870. Below, right: Figure 160. Detail from a room interior, also from "The Pictorial News," 1870.

Montclair Art Museum

IKEBANA:
JAPANESE FLOWER ARRANGEMENT

JAPANESE FLOWER ARRANGEMENT is steeped in tradition and symbolism. The roots of this ancient art can be traced back to the sixth century A.D., when Buddhism was introduced to Japan by Chinese Buddhist priests. These missionary priests brought with them beautiful T'ang ceremonial bronze vases, which they used for floral offerings. As the new religion spread many temples were built, and altar vessels were adapted from Chinese originals. The priests not only evolved a system of arranging flowers, but also developed many ways of prolonging the life of flowering material and furthered the symbolic lore associated with flowers. These early altar arrangements were known as *shin-no-hana*. Each one was arranged around a central stem or branch called *shin*, a term one meets frequently in Japanese flower arranging. In the latter part of the seventh century a famous scholar named Ono-no-Imoko, who had made three trips to China to study philosophy, government, and art, was appointed master of the Rokkakudo, Temple of Kyoto. He lived in a hermitage near a lake, within the temple grounds. Here, while arranging altar flowers in memory of his patron, he formulated certain rules of arrangement and founded the first school of this art in Japan. It became known as *Ikenobo,* which means "the priest by the lake." The school is still in existence today, its basic principles having survived all this time, and, as might be expected, many other schools have branched off from it.

From these beginnings evolved a highly stylized and formal temple art called *Rikka* or *Rikkwa.* (There is frequent confusion in the transliteration of Japanese terms.) The word actually means "standing flowers," and the kind of arrangement it describes was constructed of evergreens, foliage material, flowers, and often bare branches (Fig. 163). These arrangements were so complicated that they often took several days to complete; the branches were sometimes wired togther, and the flowers were placed in bamboo cylinders of water. Such an arrangement was extremely large, usually about six feet high; some are described as being as much as fifteen feet high and twelve feet wide, and a sixteenth-century master has remained famous for his forty-foot-high creations. These compositions initially consisted of seven branches, but further complexities brought the number up to nine and subsequently eleven; by then, *Rikka* was no longer confined to temple use but was a favorite pastime of the nobility and the upper classes. One of the underlying ideas of these arrangements was that a natural landscape should be represented in its entirety, not so much in the placing as in the combination of material selected. For instance, to display a branch of mountain cherry to the best advantage, its natural companions of the mountainside would be grouped with it. These might have included pine, since it was a dominant feature of the Japanese landscape, bamboo, cypress, cedar, camellia, and azalea. Rocks and water were not included, as the symbolism of the selected plant material made it unnecessary; pine represented the enduring quality of stone, and flowers such as white chrysanthemums could suggest cool, flowing water.

By the fifteenth century significant changes had taken place; in particular, a simpler and less complicated style of arrangement had evolved, based on the use of only three main lines, the ones we now know as "heaven," "earth," and "man," or *ten-chi-jin.* This style received its impetus from a celebrated painter Soami, who was befriended by the great

Figure 162. XIXth-century Japanese print by the artist Toyokuni showing a lady patiently coaxing a curve into flowering branches. The upright bronze vase indicates that the arrangement is to be a tall, formal one.

shogun and art patron, Yoshimasa (1436-1490). Yoshimasa had great influence on the social and artistic development of his country, for it was he who introduced the design for small houses which included the now typical household religious shrine or built-in alcove called the *tokonoma,* in which a scroll painting, a flower arrangement, and sometimes an art object were placed. He also had much to do with the perfection of the tea ceremony, or *cha-no-yu,* which became an indispensable part of Japanese life and which influenced the architecture of the home, the design of the garden, and the development of painting, as well as the creation of tea-drinking vessels. The newer school of arrangement formulated by these two men was a simplification of *Rikka* and reached its apogee in the eighteenth century. It is sometimes called *Seikwa,* sometimes *Shoka,* and frequently just *Ikenobo.*

This is only a brief sketch of the origin of the classical type of flower arrangement in Japan. There was an equally typical informal, more naturalistic style known as *Nageire,* or the "thrown-in" style. (Figs. 178 and 179.) It seems apparent that such a style existed concurrently with the ancient *Rikka* temple art and was practiced by people outside religious circles. This seemingly casual mode of flower arrangement became well known in the sixteenth century, its popularity having increased with the development of the tea cult. The simplicity of room decoration, both in public tea houses and in private homes, necessitated the use of a correspondingly simple arrangement suitable for small rooms. For such arrangements upright vases, hanging receptacles, or baskets were preferred. (Fig. 178.) Instead of exaggerated curves, the natural desire of plants to lean was emphasized. Many times arrangements slanted almost horizontally, but even so, tip ends were never allowed to droop, but seemingly aspired upward. As with the *Shoka* arrangements, they were always triangular in design, even though an exceedingly casual appearance seemed to defy the rule. This apparently artless way with flowers had great subtlety, although not all could appreciate it. The more obvious "heaven, man, and earth" or three-line arrangement continued to rival it in popularity, and for centuries, therefore, interest in the art of arranging veered between these two differing types—the classic and formal art on the one hand, and the casual and natural "thrown-in" style on the other. *Shoka,* the classic style of the Ikenobo School, reached near-perfection in the eighteenth century. Exaggerations and artificialities such as forced bending crept in during the nineteenth century, but basically the art is the same today as it was then.

With the introduction of Western customs and flowers and with the industrialization of Japan, long-time traditions have been cast aside in the twentieth century, and all the arts have undergone change. A far greater freedom of personal expression is universally indulged in. The beginning of the century saw the development of a new kind of arrangement known as *Moribana,* and there have been a number of postwar adaptations of older styles, using new ideas, but lacking definite symbolism. The *Moribana* style is purely naturalistic and was developed for use in homes built and furnished in the Western manner. It has two modes of expression; the landscape scene, made up of carefully selected branches and a few flowers (Figs. 180-85) and the grouping of cut flowers alone (Fig. 191A and E). In both instances a low, flat container is used, and at least half the water area is left exposed. The most provocative type at present is the "free form" or "abstract," a style in which every convention is cast aside, the artist frequently going outside his medium to combine unlikely materials; the results often jolt the observer to attention.

The prevalence of the practice of flower arranging over the centuries, first exclusively by the men, then by the women of Japan, is little short of amazing. There have certainly been many times in Japan's history when the emphasis on actively militaristic pursuits has seemed to dominate their civilization. However, a philosophic state of mind and a reverence for nature enabled first the priests and then the nobility and the warrior class (the *samurai*), to find tranquillity of mind and relief from life's tensions in the handling and observation of flowers. For them the important thing was in the doing, a very different attitude from that of the Occidental for whom flower arranging has been a creative activity with the purpose of providing decoration for the home. The Japanese appreciation has

Right: Figure 163. An old painting of a Rikka flower arrangement, one of a series mounted on a pair of antique folding screens. In accordance with tradition, nine differing plant materials make up the arrangement.

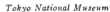

Left: Figure 164. The ancient Rikka style, arranged by Fujiwara Yuchiku of Tokyo. Mr. Yuchiku is considered the greatest living master of this style. The customary nine elements include strelitzia, cockscomb, an ilex, roses, cryptomeria, and the Easter lily. The bare branches are not identified, but the two very prominent rayed forms belong to a dracena.

New York Public Library

Courtesy: Jiro Harada

been such that great exhibitions of flower arrangements, even contests, were held as far back as the sixteenth century, and have been popular ever since. Books of instruction also date from this period. During the last half of the nineteenth century the position of women in Japan became less subordinate than in the past, and women too mastered the art of flower arranging. Indeed, so much a part of daily life did it become that innumerable schools sprang up and every young woman of good family received instruction in it as part of her education.

All Japanese flower arrangements may be divided into three basic groups.

I. Classic and formal in feeling:
   a. *Rikka* (ancient temple art)
   b. *Shoka* (asymmetrical, triangular arrangement based on three main elements known as *ten-chi-jin,* or heaven, earth, man) . This style is further broken down into: *Shin* (formal) , *Gyo* (semiformal), *So* (informal) .
II. Naturalistic and informal in character:
   a. *Nageire* (ancient and modern forms of the "thrown-in" style)
   b. *Moribana* (landscape style, or flowers alone)
III. Abstract or free-style

It should be understood that these are only general types and that there have been variations of each which have been fostered by many teachers and many schools.

Earlier in the chapter, in discussing the *Rikka* arrangements, reference was made to the underlying idea of representing nature in its entirety. If we analyze the classic *Shoka* arrangements of the Ikenobo School, which developed from the desire to simplify *Rikka,* we find that they seize what might be called an arrested moment in natural growth. To create this feeling of growth, the dynamic, rhythmic motion of clear, unconfused line is

126

Opposite page, left: Figure 165. Traditional Shoka arrangement, Shin style, of the Ikenobo School. Blue iris are placed in a tall classic bronze container. The red lacquer board bears the gold crest the school awards its instructors. Arrangement by Mary C. Takahashi. Opposite page, right: Figure 166. Semiformal Gyo style of Ikenobo, arranged by Miss Haruko Hamada. Of great interest is the twisted branch, cut and placed to add needed weight and stability to the slim stems of the plant material. Note how the recurved tip of the tallest placement is just over the place where the stems emerge from the water.

Figure 167. Informal So style of Ikenobo arrangement by Mrs. Yoneo Arai. Mrs. Arai's school of Enshu-ryu is one of the oldest and best-known schools of classic flower arrangement. It formed the basis for Josiah Conder's books, written during the last century, on the floral art of Japan. The flowing lines of these artificially curved branches, with their emphasis on the horizontal thrust of the Tai placement, are typical of this school and the informal style of So. The daffodils in the low dish fall into the same classification.

Figure 168. A New Year's print, called a Surimono, by the artist Itchinsai Utagawa. The elaborately curled Japanese aspidistra leaves place the arrangement immediately as belonging to the nineteenth century, when exaggerations in style were commonplace. An informal Ikenobo arrangement.

always evident. The irregularities of old, gnarled, windswept trees, the traceries of bare branches against the sky, and all such dramatic instances of nature's draughtsmanship, are felt and viewed again in the idealized groupings of plant material in vases. This appreciation of fine line design is also to be seen in Japanese prints, especially those of the great eighteenth-century masters, as well as in the postures and the flowing costumes of the *Noh* dramas.

Stems, foliage, buds, and blossoms are included in such arrangements in order to spell out the entire character of a plant, and it is considered important to re-create the way blossoms and foliage turn toward the sun and the tips of plants turn up to the light. In Japanese flower arranging, the onlooker is considered to be in the position of the sun, and the elements of an arrangement must look up or out toward the viewer. There are a few conventions which are always followed in order to gain naturalness in the illusion of growth. The first of these might be called the convention of timeliness. Flowers are never used out of season; and as timeliness is always expressed in their choice, bare branches appear only in the late fall and winter, and branches with certain sweeping curves are used in March to suggest the winds. The amount of water showing in a container is also linked with the seasons. Low vases with large water areas are favored for summer or the time of spring floods, and during these seasons the top pan of a *usubata*, a classic bronze vase (Fig. 176) is always filled when in use. A second convention is that the height-relationships in nature should be observed. Therefore, a tree branch is always placed higher in an arrangement than a flower or shrub which would naturally be shorter; and mountain plants are used above field flowers.

One other technique which adds very greatly to the illusion of growth is that of super-imposing flower or branch stems, as they emerge from a container, for four or five inches (Fig. 177). This gives a satisfying feeling of stability and, in cases when branches rather

128

than flower stems are used, can give the effect of a tree trunk. Frequently the Japanese superimpose separate pieces of branches at this point, if extra visual weight seems needed (Fig. 166).

The two obvious characteristics of the classic *Shoka* arrangement are asymmetrical design and emphasis on line. Since symmetrical shapes rarely exist in growing plants and trees, the Japanese long ago established a balance of inequalities in their flower art, so that an uneven number of elements always makes up the three component parts of such arrangements. The beautifully related proportions of these parts are worked out with unerring skill, the arranger assembling the arrangement in his hands first, before making any placements in a container. The tallest line is called *Shin*. It is always at least one and a half times the height of the container and may even reach three times the height. A gentle curve is often forced into it if it did not have one to begin with, and in order to gain perfect balance the tip of the branch must appear directly over the spot where the stem comes out of the water. The intermediate line is called *Soe* and should be two-thirds the length of the *Shin* line, while the lowest placement, or *Tai*, is two-thirds the

Figure 169. Cherry blossoms in a boat-shaped gourd. An informal Ikenobo arrangement with a feeling of sailing, arranged by Mrs. Yoneo Arai.

length of the *Soe* line. These placements were thought of as "heaven, man, and earth," but with some confusion resulting from the fact that the Ikenobo School considered "Heaven" to be on the horizon and it therefore designated the middle element as such. With such rigid rules it would seem that these arrangements might be tiresomely alike, but actually great variation is possible within the confines of the triangle which is formed by the imaginary lines drawn through the tips of the branches. According to the height of the arrangement, the proportions of the triangle change, and of course there is infinite variety in plant material. A rather quaint idea is expressed in the invariable *Shoka* custom of having two of the basic lines or elements of the design face in toward each other. The Japanese say, "Flowers like to talk to each other."

In the past, three main types of *Shoka* arrangements were made. The tall and formal ones which made use of flowers just as they grew naturally formed a subclassification or style called *Shin*. No artificial bending or coaxing of curves was used, although excess material was pruned, as it always is in every arrangement.

The *Shin* type of arrangement appears in upright vases of bronze or pottery. A semiformal classification, called *Gyo*, was made up of gently curving stems placed in broader, upright vases of medium height, such as a *usubata* or a basket. The *So* style of arrangement had sweeping lines produced by forced bending and took on an informality and a horizontal emphasis. Vases for this style were varied and included low bronze or pottery receptacles called *suibans*, bamboo cylinders (some double-tiered), pottery "boats," hanging bamboo "boats," "moons," and gourds.

Figure 170. The basket arrangement on this embroidered cushion shows the use of Nejime in Ikenobo arrangement. Willow branches blowing in the wind are combined with a single camellia, which has been substituted for a low "earth" placement of willow. The basket and the double-tiered bamboo vase are typical containers for informal (So style) Ikenobo arrangements. This and the next illustration are part of an eighteenth-century writing-box set.

Figure 171. Three vases typical of the informal So style of Iken-obo were used on this embroidered cushion. The hanging bamboo boat was always a popular type of container, and flowers placed in it could be made to represent outgoing or incoming boats. The water arrangement of iris reveals the flowers' way of growth, and the gourd hangs on a post in the manner in which they are still used at the side of the tokonoma.

Forced bending of branches must be done patiently but firmly; it is best accomplished by thumb pressure with a bearing-down motion of the fourth and little fingers. A slightly twisting motion is some insurance against breaking, but the main thing to guard against is exerting pressure at a joint. Sometimes running hot water over the stems makes them more pliable. The Japanese are adept at sawing partially through a branch and inserting a tiny wedge into the opening, thereby obtaining exaggerated curves. The arrangement of pussy willow shown in Fig. 167 is a fine example of the sweeping curves that with patience can be coaxed from plant material. A wood-block print intended for a New Year's card (Fig. 168) shows the extremes to which the art of flower arrangement succumbed in the nineteenth century.

Interest and charm has been added to these arrangements through the frequent combination of flowers and branches. The flowers could replace the entire "earth" or *Tai* placement (Fig. 175) or could be superimposed as a separate three-part arrangement on the main one, or could even be placed a little apart. Such placements are called *Nejime*. Traditionally, classic arrangements seldom deviated from the custom of being made of only one kind of plant material or at most of a combination of two kinds. Three kinds of plant material were grouped together only when the container was a two-tiered, cylindrical, bamboo vase, in which case the entire grouping was often supposed to represent a whole landscape of mountain and meadowland. Therefore material from the mountain top, its slopes, and the land below was included; such a group might then have been made up of pine, camellia, and flowers such as daffodils or chrysanthemums.

To hold flower stems or branches in place, ingenious forked twigs wedged across vase openings, about an inch below the rim, have always been used in the classical

131

arrangements. These are called *kubari*. Stems placed in the opening of the fork were further secured with a crosspiece known as a *komi*, and since they were set at a diagonal, their ends were always cut slantwise so as to fit snugly against the inside of the vase. For the flat and open containers, ingenious metal holders in the form of rings, turtles, crabs, fish, and even scissors have been used. When the holder was not a decorative one, pebbles or small stones usually covered it. The pin holder, or *kenzan*, is favored for *Moribana* arrangements.

Stands or bases are frequently placed beneath flower vases and form part of any completed arrangement. They not only seem to put the finishing touch to the arrangement but they add visual weight for perfect balance; they also perform a utilitarian function in protecting the floor of the *tokonoma* (the alcove) or table top. The Japanese love of irregularity is seen in their preference for placing rectangular stands under round vases and round or irregularly shaped bases under rectangular containers.

Certain clearly formulated Japanese rules for arrangement were taken up by American flower arrangers when they first began to seek out some already established principles. These have since become a standard part of our arranging techniques. The rule of proportion of flower to vase (one and a half times the height) has become the first and most favored rule, very frequently followed literally, but more successfully used as a general guide. The beauty of outline or silhouette is appreciated when crossed lines or parallel stems are eliminated and when there is variety in the shapes of the empty spaces between design elements. It is important in both Japanese and American types of arranging to make all placements uneven in height. One thing that Americans are apt to forget is that the Japanese classic flower arrangements were meant to be viewed at eye level, since the Japanese knelt in front of the low alcove platform where the arrangement was placed.

To emphasize the spirit in which these arrangements were created and viewed, I quote from a book written for Yamanaka and Co. by Professor Ohashi. He gives the following directions for viewing arranged flowers: "Sit properly about three feet away from *Tokonoma* and bow gently. Look first into lower part and glance upward. If one cares to see the roots and ground about, bow again then quietly crawl up to *Tokonoma* and placing two hands on your knees, gently look in. In all cases, criticism and rough movement are to be refrained." Since the American mode of living was recognized to be entirely different, the author added that it would be "sufficient if students could realize the spirit thereof." Flowers brought by guests made the one exception to the rule that arrangements should be placed at eye level. These were placed in hanging vases or wall receptacles so that they could be "looked up to."

Because the Japanese have been so intimately acquainted with their natural surroundings and have sought to re-create pictures in nature with their plant materials, it has not been their custom to force blooms out of season. The commonplace materials have been the best-loved ones. Their gardens, which have brought the essence of mountains, water, rocks, and valleys close at hand, have made use of cultivated flowers only in the old Chinese manner. Potted plants just ready to blossom were occasionally placed in the ground to be admired until the cycle of their development was completed. In country areas, flowers for arrangement have always been easily obtained, but city dwellers have been dependent on the flower vendors with their pushcarts. Making the rounds of the cities each day, these peddlers supplied the flowers which always have been considered a necessity for indoor use, not alone for beauty's sake but as a traditional part of holidays and religious festivals and as a courtesy in the entertainment of guests.

Heading the list of favorite flowers is, quite naturally, the chrysanthemum. Known to the Japanese for centuries, it has been developed into a flower which blooms the year round and which has become not only a national symbol but a greatly venerated art motive. There is no occasion when its use is unsuitable. It appears in many combinations— in contrast with branches of pine, as a foil for branches of cypress or pussy willow, and

Figure 172. *A modern interpretation of the old style, using modern plant materials. Trimmed palmetto leaves are used with coconut fibers. The two groups, so perfectly related to each other, are separated by a small space which the Japanese call "the place where the fish swim through." Arrangement by Mrs. Yoneo Arai.*

Above: Figures 173, 174, 175. Three steps in a classic Shoka arrangement of broom and tansy. The tansy is substituted for an "earth" or Tai placement of broom and is referred to as Nejime. Far left: Figure 176. A forked stick, or kubari, cut to fit the vase opening tightly, is the usual Japanese flower holder for classic arrangements. Left: Figure 177. The alignment of stems, front to back, gives the feeling of a single placement when viewed from the front.

as one of the group of "the four friends," namely chrysanthemum, bamboo, plum, and orchid. The pine, the bamboo, and the early plum are a favorite combination in Japan, just as they are in China; and another group of plant materials that one sees frequently is that of the so-called "seven flowers of autumn," a combination which includes grasses as well as flowers. The *Iris Kaempferi*, the red or white camellia, and the paper-white narcissus have all been popular for flower arrangements. Even the lowly aspidistra, which seems commonplace to our eyes, has yielded beautiful design. Strangely enough, even though many beautiful lilies are native to Japan, few except the orange wood lily and the "Easter" lily (*Lilium longiflorum*) have found their way into vases, for their flamboyant character has not been appreciated by the Japanese.

To this people, all plant life has had sexual attributes, the flowers and grasses being thought of as female and the trees as male. Colors too are distinguished in this manner, the masculine colors being the strong, vibrant ones of red, purple, and pink, whereas white and the softer hues of blue and yellow are considered feminine. With the exception of white flowers, which top the list in importance, the masculine flowers always hold the dominant positions in arrangements. Fully opened flowers also belong to this category, but buds are feminine.

This is necessarily but a brief glimpse of the history and the classic styles of Japanese flower arranging. We Westerners can absorb this art of the Japanese up to a point and take joy in practicing it; but the state of mind with which a Japanese has always approached it, along with its underlying philosophy and complex symbolism, combine to make it something that we can never embrace in its entirety.

The last fifty years have seen the development of *Moribana*, which in translation means either "piles of flowers in a bowl" or "massed flowers." Prerequisite to this style is the use of a low, flat container called a *suiban*. Established in 1910 by the flower master Unshin Ohara with the explicit purposes of breaking away from the rigidity of the past and using the new and more colorful flowers from the West, it has made a great contribution in its delightful representations of naturalistic landscapes or "memory sketches." These realistic small scenes conjure up far, middle, or near views and all materials are seasonal companions of similar habitat. Thus there are mountain, water, or meadow scenes. These are often made of branches representing gnarled trees and of small flowers, and separate placements are often made instead of all elements emerging together from one place. The branches are usually cut in the proportion of one and a half times the width (not the length) of the container. According to the season an expanse of water is allowed to show, and if the chosen plant material includes some water-loving plants, moss, or stones, a whole scene in nature is conjured up in the eyes of the beholder. Another expression of

Left: Figure 178. A wall arrangement in the "thrown-in" style of Nageire, made by Sofu Teshigahara, Tokyo. Right: Figure 179. A contemporary arrangement in the Nageire or "thrown-in" style. Arranged by Mrs. Jiro Harada, Tokyo.

Photo: Roche

Figures 180 to 183. Paintings of Moribana arrangements, three in the landscape style and one with flowers grouped naturalistically. Note that the use of three main component parts is still adhered to and that the expanse of water that shows in each arrangement is a featured part of the design.

Figure 184. A natural-scenery Moribana arrangement called shakei. This is a late winter scene made up of club moss, narcissus, winter chrysanthemums, pine, and rose hips. Because of the season no water is apparent.

Figure 185. Moribana spring-time arrangement of flowering branches, rape, and club moss. Rape is a forage crop (one of the brassicas) widely grown in Japan.

Figure 186. A Japanese lady arranging mallow blossoms before a basket container already in place on the floor of the alcove.

Moribana makes use of flowers only (Fig. 180), with their own foliage, and in this case they are usually colorful, short-stemmed, and grouped by kind. Again, there is an expanse of water left to view. Analysis will show that both types are still built around the triangle and that three main placements are always evident, though in massed groupings of flowers the triangle is three-dimensional, and to see it we must look down on the arrangement. The three main elements of all *Moribana* designs are referred to as "subject line," "secondary line," and "object line," instead of heaven, man, and earth. The other parts are referred to as "subsidiary lines."

Just before World War II there were a number of manifestations by the masters of *Ikebana* which pointed the way to a complete revolution in the art. In 1930, perhaps challenged by the freedom of painters and sculptors who had embraced such things as surrealism, and abstraction, a real declaration of independence was issued by a group of flower masters in a document which stated in part, "We reject the botanical restriction of flowers. We embrace a free use of containers. We are revolutionary to an extreme and are therefore without fixed form. We are, however, concerned with the styles of modern living and we have strong artistic consciences. Our task is entirely different from that of earlier flower arrangers. We must express a new image in a new spirit."

In the aftermath of war, in an age of rapid change, violence, and materialism, all the arts—painting, sculpture, architecture, and literature—in Japan, in Europe, and in America have gone through convulsive transformations. Art expressions must have quick impact, be novel, exciting, colorful, even ugly. Subtlety seldom exists. "Free-style" or *"avant-garde"* flower arrangements combine flowers with feathers, plastic, glass, rope, and other nonfloral materials, and make use of such elements as vines and branches stripped of their bark and painted. Branches are placed upside down over vases (Fig. 192), lines of design are intermingled crosswise or are paralleled, even numbers of flowers are used, stems are contorted and twisted. Containers are often free-form, very coarse-textured and crude, exotic in shape, and have an affinity with the work of contemporary sculpture. Such individualistic expressions are not inappropriate to the modern scene. It must be reiterated that the Japanese home has become Westernized and the *tokonoma* is no longer the sole repository for flowers. Contemporary dining and living rooms, foyers, offices, hotel lobbies, and department stores all display arrangements, and with the rise of numerous flower-arrangement schools which have thousands of pupils, exhibitions are frequently held.

While there are many schools of *Ikebana* and many teaching masters in Japan today, three masters and their schools have emerged as the most influential. These are *Ikenobo*, *Ohara*, and *Sogetsu*. Of longest standing is the ancient Ikenobo School, whose headmaster, or *iemoto*, is Senei Ikenobo, the forty-fifth in the line of succession from father to son. Naturally this school has not given up all its age-old traditions, and *Shoka*, the classic asymmetrical, heaven-earth-man arrangement based on the triangle, is still taught. Now, however, it is most generally created with three kinds of plant material instead of one or two. Both old and modern forms of *Rikka, Nageire,* and *Moribana* are taught, the modernizations making use of the newer nonplant materials and allowing the arranger free self-expression. The Ikenobo Institute, situated both in Tokyo and Kyoto, has hundreds of pupils, taught in classes instead of individually in the home.

Figure 187. An interesting contemporary expression that makes use of seven different plant materials, just as in the ancient Rikka style. Although symbolism is noticeably absent from most present-day Japanese arrangements, the artist, Kikushu Hasegawa of Kyoto, explained that he purposely selected dead as well as living material, berries as well as flowers, for this arrangement.

Photo: **Boutrelle**

Figure 188

Photo: Boutrelle

Figures 188 and 189. Two modern Japanese arrangements by Sofu Teshigahara of Tokyo. Mr. Teshigahara has founded a new school called Sogetsu, which exemplifies a postwar tendency to break with the past.

Figure 190. A sensitively portrayed free-style expression of fall featuring pome-
granates, lotus leaves, and the winter chrysanthemum. Arranged by the Head-
master of the Ohara School, Houn Ohara.

A.

B.

C.

D.

E.

Figure 191. The five basic styles of the Ohara School.
A. *A Moribana color study in the upright style.*
B. *Slanting style (Heika, tall-vase method).*
C. *Cascade style (Moribana low-bowl method).*
D. *Contrasting style (Heika).*
E. *Vertical or Heavenly style (Moribana).*

The school with the largest pupil enrollment is the Sogetsu School, which claims over a million students in Japan and abroad. Its founder was Sofu Teshigahara—still the headmaster. In 1926, in an attempt to broaden the uses of flower arrangement and get it out of the *tokonoma*, he initiated the imaginative free style, which he likens to sculpture, with flowers and nonvegetal materials the medium. Compositions of stone, scrap metal, feathers, shells, glass, etc., are designed three dimensionally, and spray-painted natural plant materials may or may not be added. Containers often have a decidedly sculptural effect, some being coarse-textured and unconventional in shape. Sometimes none is used. The school believes, however, that complete freedom obtains only after discipline is learned and that a fundamental knowledge of the old styles is still necessary. Therefore *Nageire* and *Moribana* are still taught; they also serve to provide the student with technique.

Sogetsu arrangements are not infrequently made by combining the low *Moribana* and the tall-vased *Nageire* into one composition, a new and very effective idea. The basic *Moribana, Nageire,* and combined styles are taught in both upright and slanting styles but two methods of approach are emphasized. The traditional one expresses the natural beauty of the plant material; the newer free-style approach expresses the individual. Such a decidedly contemporary appeal has made this the most popular school in present-day Japan.

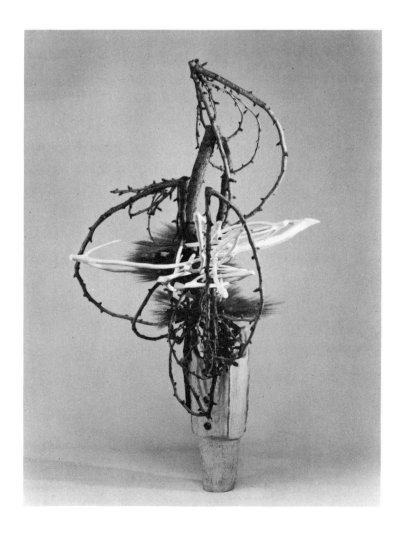

Figure 192. Contemporary freestyle arrangement of the Ohara School.

144

Figure 193. Free-style arrangement in an unconventional container. Perfect balance has been achieved between the large trimmed monstera leaf and the vase itself.

The Ohara School, now presided over by Houn Ohara, the grandson of the founder, has a number of branches not only in Japan but also in America. It has retained its natural-scenery *Moribana*, called Shakei, but has revitalized the *Moribana* which emphasized color and texture, by using contemporary vases. Teaching has been formalized into five basic styles, using the standard three main elements, as follows: (Figs. 191A-E)

1. Upright
2. Slanting (The object stem, or tallest element, extends outward instead of upward)
3. Cascade (The object or main stem cascades from the vase and must go below the rim of the container)
4. Contrasting (The object and secondary stems extend outward opposite each other and at slightly different levels and are uneven in length)
5. Vertical or Heavenly (A tall narrow triangle is formed)

All these styles may be adapted to both the *Moribana* low-vase method or the *Heika* tall-vase method. They must be learned well before pupils are allowed to advance to the free-style arrangements, in which convention is tossed aside and individual expression takes over. Always the guiding principle is that there be complete freedom in showing off the true beauty and dominant characteristic of the flowers used. It is thought that the nature of plant material can be further enhanced away from its natural setting.

145

The influence of these Japanese expressions upon Western flower arrangers has been considerable. It has been fostered by the organization called Ikebana International, whose various chapters have many paying members who take lessons from teachers sent out from Japan, who stage exhibitions, and who are privileged to attend demonstrations by the various masters of flower arrangement who go on tour. There is no doubt that Japan's modern floral expressions are the most stimulating and the most provocative in the world today.

Figure 194. A delicately beautiful modern Rikka arrangement of the Ikenobo School.

Figure 195. Free-style arrangement of the Ohara School. For modern work the Japanese are fond of using bleached materials. Especially favored are edgeworthia branches, frequently used inverted. They are combined here with gerbera blossoms.

146

Heika	(Hay-kah)	Name of upright type of arrangement used by Ohara School
Ikebana	(Ee-kay-bah-nah)	The art of flower arrangement
Ikenobo	(Ee-kay-no-bo)	The original seventh-century school of flower arrangement founded by Ono-no-Imoko, "the priest by the lake." Now the term generally applied to traditional three-part heaven-man-earth style
Kakemono	(Kah-kay-mo-no)	A scroll painting
Kenzan	(Ken-ann)	A needle point flower holder
Komi	(Ko-mee)	The crosspiece used with *kubari* to hold flowers in place in vase
Kubari	(Kuh-bah-ree)	A Y-shaped piece of wood, which when fitted inside the neck of a vase serves as a flower holder
Moribana	(Mor-ee-bah-nah)	Twentieth-century types of arrangement. Of two kinds, naturalistic landscapes or colorful flowers. Originated by Unshin Ohara
Nageire	(Nah-gay-ee-reh)	"Thrown-in" style of arrangement
Nejime	(Neh-gee-meh)	One flower or a group used as lowest placement in an *Ikenobo* arrangement of flowerless branches. It is a substitute for bottom *Tai* placement
Nemoto	(Neh-mo-to)	That section in an arrangement, between the lowest placement and the water, where the stems are superimposed
Ohara	(Oh-hah-ra)	School founded in early years of twentieth century by Unshin Ohara, who originated the *Moribana* style
Rikka	(Rik-kah)	Ancient temple art of flower arrangement. Means "standing flowers"
Seika	(Say-kah)	Name for the classic *Ikenobo* type of arrangement. See *Shoka*
Shakei	(Sha-kay)	*Moribana* landscape style of the Ohara school
Shin	(Shin)	Main central branch of three-part arrangement
Shin-no-hana	(Shin-no-hah-nah)	The earliest type of Japanese altar flower arrangement. Sixth century
Shoka	(Sho-kah)	A name for the classic *Ikenobo* three-part arrangement. See *Seika*
Soe	(So-ae)	Intermediate branch, or group, of three-part arrangement
Sogetsu	(So-gait-sue)	Twentieth-century school, largest in Japan. Founded in 1926 by Sofu Teshigahara. For the most part freedom of expression is stressed, but traditional styles are also taught
Tai	(Ty-ee)	Lowest branch, or group, of three-part arrangement
Ten-chi-jin	(Ten-chee-geen)	"Heaven-earth-man" arrangement
Tokonoma	(To-ko-noh-mah)	The alcove in the Japanese home in which are placed a hanging scroll, a flower arrangement, and often a precious ornament

147

Figure 196. The magnificent Magnolia grandiflora displayed like a solitaire. The sweep of added foliage gives perfectly balanced line, height, and grace. Arranged by Marie Johnson Fort.

CONTEMPORARY ARRANGEMENTS

1952

AFTER EXAMINING past ways with flowers, it is interesting to analyze the flower arrangements of the present with special attention to historical influences. In a general way, contemporary arrangements may be said to fall into three classifications or types. Those which are full or profuse and which display either a massed grouping of one kind of flower and foliage or a variety of many forms, colors and textures, we call *mass* arrangements. The bouquet art of Europe has found its modern expression here. The arrangements which stress silhouette, outline shapes, and a dynamic line in their design, using but a selective amount of plant material, are referred to as *line* arrangements. This form of expression has, of course, stemmed directly from the Orient, particularly from Japan. Its dramatic simplicity is stimulating both to behold and to create; yet in other moods, the inner satisfaction of dealing with or of viewing vibrant colors or subtle tones in massed groupings is equally gratifying.

The third type of arrangement is a combination of the first two. This mingling of two basic contrasting ways of handling flowers seems to express the creative attainment of today's American flower arrangers. Strong lines or forms of design, filled in or emphasized by flowering material and foliage, and frequently combined with accessories, make what can be called our typical arrangement. This is usually referred to as a *line-mass* grouping. The variety of self-expression that may be attained in this type of grouping is really impressive.

A group of photographs of contemporary work is included here to illustrate these three types of arrangement. At best it can be but a sampling of available examples, for of course there are many hundreds from which to choose. This selection, however, has been carefully made and should serve as a basis for the evaluation of other present day flower arrangements.

I hope that the reader may forgive a little editorializing here. The writer has acted as a judge at many flower shows and has made mental note of certain rather universal pitfalls. There seems to be an unfortunate inclination to stuff so many flower-heads together that they look smothered, "mashed" rather than "massed." As a result, we see flat, uninteresting surfaces, rather than surfaces broken up by the angles of individual flowers, some pulled slightly forward and others turned slightly sideways. As someone once put it so well to me, "To show off to best advantage, flowers should have *nodding room!*"

Many readers will also agree with me in decrying the tendency toward over-stylization, which results in stiff, labored-looking arrangements that express too literally the two verbs one sees so often in writings on the subject—*build* and *construct*. Flower arrangement includes more of esthetics and less of engineering than that!

Therefore a study of the masters of painting is immensely valuable. Their combinations of flowers may have been at times unnatural, but never their delineation of the flowers themselves. They were careful, always, to preserve the inherent qualities of line and form that each flower possesses.

To what may the present rather self-conscious tendency be ascribed?

Possibly we are losing touch with one of the most gratifying experiences that is to be had in the handling of flowers—their cultivation. Do all flower arrangers today grow at least some of the flowers they handle? To be a real artist one must know all the inherent qualities of the chosen medium. There must be knowledge of and respect for all its innate possibilities. The ceramic artist mixes his own glazes and fires his own pieces in order to achieve the ultimate in his particular field. The true artist of the camera develops and prints his own photographs in order to capture all the tonal subtleties of black and white. If one has grown one's own flowers, watered them, and tended them with care, how *can* one place them in vases and force them into the exaggerated poses in which they are only too often displayed?

Let us re-examine the natural ease and grace of Europe's bouquets, as well as the discernment and refinement of the Far East, as seen by the great artists. Therein lies fresh and infinite inspiration.

1968

In the short space of fifteen years there have been marked changes in flower arranging, due primarily to the dominant role the major flower shows play. Their awards establish styles. Keeping in step with contemporary painters and sculptors, garden club flower

Figure 197. A variety of garden roses combined in a horizontal arrangement for a living or dining room table. Grace and delicacy were stressed. The gradation of color ranged from the very pale pink of the clustered polyantha roses known as the Fairy to the deepest rose of the center blooms. Arranged by the author.

Roche

Left: Figure 198. A large arrangement of massed wild flowers finds a perfect setting on an outdoor terrace. Arranged by Mary Alice Roche.

Opposite page: Figure 199. A graceful, urn-shaped container is usually a good choice for a mass arrangement. The wide mouth takes many flowers easily, and the pedestal base adds dignity and proportion. Branches of Philadelphus, single white peonies, and white-margined funkia leaves are arranged here by the author.

arrangers are following modern trends in the world of art. All are seeking to interpret the modern environment typified by the feeling of tension, brutality, speed, and materialism. This is what the Japanese were experimenting with in the 1930's, what Americans have been doing for the last ten years, and what the British are now beginning to accept. It is rare indeed, in America, to see quantities of flowers arranged *en masse,* although the English bouquet, gracefully elevated, is still typical of that country. For exhibition work traditional styles are *passé* and the emphasis seems to be on *"much from little and let your imagination soar."* Free-style creations, abstracts, mobiles, and assemblages, even today's "minimal art" are all looked upon as appropriate expressions of the flower arranger, leaving the public often bewildered because of the scarcity of flowers and because compositions are seldom "pretty." Much of the exhibition work is stylish, striking, and clever, some is downright ugly, and the containers are often crude in the extreme; but though beauty is frequently denied, design is always present.

Yesterday's flower-show work achieved modernity through exaggeration, perhaps through attenuated height; through contrast in texture and color; and through the use of plant materials considered to be exotic. Themes were taken from our direct experience of the world around us and translated into interpretive arrangements. Today abstract expression is the inspiration for many flower-show arrangements. In these, the essence of subject matter is distilled and rational relationships are discarded.

Successful contemporary creations call for a basic knowledge of design used with acute sensibility to the demands of perfect balance. One immediately rejects an off-balance composition, since it is psychologically disturbing, and nowhere is lack of balance more apparent than in free-style art and in abstractions composed of few parts. Of the other component principles of design—scale, proportion, rhythm, harmony, dominance, contrast, and silhouette—the last two seem now to outweigh the others in importance. Contrasts of smooth and rough textures and of dull and intense colors, in both vase and plant material, and of the lines and planes of foliage and flowers are played against each other. Much is made of space being deliberately opened up within a design, perhaps dividing it in two, and whereas traditionally styled arrangements reach out into space and create irregular silhouettes, it is now common practice to enclose space with bent reeds and inverted branches in order to design with unconventional new shapes—a conceit first employed by the Japanese.

When nonorganic things such as feathers, rope, rock, shells, and plastic, as well as salvage from the junkyard are composed with plant material, usually with a minimum of

flowers, we have the assemblage. Truck and bed springs and parts of washing machines have all been used, and the total effort rather frequently falls into the category of what we call "pop" art. It is to be hoped that this trend will be transient, for floral beauty cannot long remain denied by true flower-lovers. It has seemed more than strange for members of garden clubs, who supposedly do garden, to be eager to work with such a paucity of flowering material. Perhaps we should stop applying the term "flower arranging" to these creations and think of them only as decorative compositions.

Since flowers are now used so sparingly each one is chosen with special regard for its size and shape, with color usually of secondary importance. The large rounds of dahlias, chrysanthemums, and sometimes of carnations and roses; the trumpets of lilies, the spikes of gladioli and torch ginger, and the striking shapes and colors of strelitzia, anthurium, and the calla lily are almost monotonously used in combination with large leaves of interesting texture or outline. Mutilated leaves and painted vines and branches add interest, but there is relatively little variety when one considers the very many charming and more delicate flowers which are not adaptable to modern show work.

It would not be fair to close this chapter without stating that within the home, in the church, at the club, or in the decoration of special places for special occasions we do find a nice handling of flowers and greens in a natural and traditional way and that floral beauty still abounds. But it is sadly true that a large cutting garden is almost a thing of the past in America. Because of lack of hired help and generally smaller home grounds, people do have fewer flowers at hand and become more and more dependent upon buying them and upon seeking the maximum effect from just a few.

Where we go from here is hard to tell. The modern abstraction most certainly has a place in the modern home and in some of the classes of the flower show, while the traditional mass, line-mass, or line arrangement suits the traditional home. But the slavish following of every modern art cult puts flower arrangement in the category of mere diversion and prevents it from being recognized as the unique art form it really is—a transient, living one.

Figure 200. "Monday's child is fair of face." An interpretive arrangement made by Mrs. Robert N. Graham. A very subtle relationship of textures was achieved with the use of white stock, camellias, and Easter lilies in combination with the alabaster and marble container and figure.

Figure 201. A midsummer mass arrangement with intensely blue hydrangeas, delphiniums, white lilies, and yellow-centered chrysanthemums resembling Shasta daisies. Full bouquets are usually best displayed in footed containers such as this oversized goblet; a low vase often seems oppressed by the weight of its contents. It was important, in this crystal container, to rely on the visual weight of exposed stems as a counterbalance to the large grouping, so that the flowers would not appear to be falling out of the vase. Arrangement by the author.

Photo: Roche

Figure 202. An interpretative composition by the author called "The North wind doth blow and we shall have snow." Branches of hackberry, deformed by a mishap of nature referred to as witches'-broom, were arranged in a stark outline and sprayed with artificial snow.

Photo: Sheldon

Photo: Roche

Above: Figure 203. "Clear and Windy," an unusual silhouette arrangement of great distinction because of its imagination and stark simplicity. The clever introduction of red gloriosa lilies not only provided a colorful focal point but helped further in carrying out the feeling of windswept motion. Arranged by Mrs. E. Bartlett Headden.

Right: Figure 204. A line of design provided by branches of foliage material often proves to be the best starting point for a flower arrangement. The addition of flowers will round out the arrangement, point up the principles of good design, and add colorful interest. Arrangement by Mrs. Kenneth D. Smith.

Figure 205. A strikingly handsome design worked out by Mrs. William H. Barton for the challenging modern ceramic container. Emphasis is strictly upon form and texture; but exquisite balance is achieved in the placement of agave and ficus foliage, palm spathes, artichokes, and bananas.

Figure 206. *A striking arrangement which features both outline silhouette and textures. Skillful designing has provided a strong focal point at the place where the oppositional thrust of two dominant lines meet. Arranged by Mrs. George J. Hirsch.*

Figure 207. The long-recognized "line of beauty," or S-curve, provides the line of design upon which this arrangement is based. When handled with skill, the pliable stems and curled buds and flowers of the calla lily fall easily into this pattern. Arranged by Mrs. George Hamilton Davis.

Opposite: Figure 208. The brilliant flowers in this typical English bouquet form a loose triangular mass. The delicate shapes of lily-flowered tulips and their open placement keep it from becoming too heavy. Clivia blossoms effect a subtle color graduation between the red and yellow flowers. Arranged by Julia Clements.

Photo: Boutrelle

Photo: Jon Whitbourne

Photo: Roche

Figure 210. The ethereal beauty of lycoris blossoms displayed in a "toasting goblet" whose air-twist stem seems like a fairy's wand. Curving stems and tendrils of the stephanotis vine further the feeling of delicacy and grace. A pin-holder, too large to stand on the bottom of the cup, rested about three-quarters of the way down, leaving a clear space for the light to gleam through the crystal. Arrangement by Anne Elizabeth Erhorn.

Opposite page: Figure 209. A deceptively simple arrangement, composed entirely of marigolds. Lines of design were set up first by the placement of the slender, bud-bearing stems. Flowers were added next, skillfully placed to avoid any confusion of line. There is beautiful silhouette and necessary weight at the focal point. A real feeling of third dimension exists because of the manner in which the flower heads have been placed, some tucked back into the arrangement and others pulled forward. Arranged by Mrs. Harold Brooks.

Opposite: Figure 211. A composition stressing a sweeping line of design but created to interpret the flower show theme "wood-carving." The designer carved the graceful bird and chose the right textured plant material, strelitzia blossoms and leaves, to carry out the theme. Simple blocks of wood and the tools of the carver completed the arrangement. Mrs. T. Bromley Flood.

Right: Figure 212. A very slender S-curve, starting with the topmost piece of wheat and working down through the tip of the rake, provides the line interest here, while the rich, warm tones of the massed chrysanthemums and fruit give a clear-cut and orderly aspect to this distinguished arrangement by Mrs. William Joy.

Photo: Boutrelle

Figure 213. An interpretive abstraction of the theme "indecision" could almost be called minimal art; there are so few parts. Bleached, knotted, and painted Japanese wisteria was placed in such a manner that the composition had balance and carefully planned space relationships. Mrs. Raymond Russ Stoltz.

*Figure 214. Bent forsythia canes forming varied spatial shapes substituted for foliage in this arrangement, and their stark **outlines** contrasted knowingly with the greater complexity of the orchids. Placed in an earth-colored container, they were displayed against a "burnt orange" woolen material. Mrs. Charles F. Hoell.*

Figure 216. Only three aspidistra leaves and two pears created this arresting design. Perfectly balanced and displayed against a white background, it had impact through contrast and restraint. Mrs. Harry C. Groome, Jr.

Photo: Edmund B. Gilchrist, Jr.

Figure 217. An assemblage called "Sunflower" was staged against a yellow background. Black-painted bamboo stalks, a wall-clock frame, a plow disc, and a wooden stand created a starkly modern outline, and a pandanus fruit pod furthered the sunflower motif. Strelitzia added more color and drama. Mrs. Rae L. Goldson.

Figure 218. A flower-show class required the use of stained glass, and the exhibitor designed a Mondrianesque composition combining orange and red pieces of glass, black wooden dowels, red and orange roses, and a minimum of glycerinized foliage. In 1963 it was of the very moment. Mrs. John F. Hayes.

Fig. 219. An arrangement called "Contemporary Contrasts" was strongly influenced by present-day Japanese expressions. In its execution the opposing stresses of horizontal and vertical lines of thorn were stabilized by the upright thrust of the vase and flowers. Mrs. John W. Knight, Jr.

Photo: Lewis Henderson

A SOURCE LIST OF GARDEN FLOWERS

DUTCH AND FLEMISH
Seventeenth and Eighteenth Centuries

This list has been compiled by the author, who has identified these plant materials from Dutch and Flemish flower paintings of the seventeenth and eighteenth centuries.

FLOWERING MATERIALS [1]

Alkanet or Bugloss [Anchusa officinalis]
Allium Moly
Aloe
Anemone [A. coronaria], single, double; red, purple, white, variegated
Apple
Artichoke
Auricula [Primula auricula]
Autumn Crocus [Colchicum]
Calendula
Carnation, pink, red, white, bi-color
Christmas Rose [Helleborus]
Chrysanthemum [C. sinense], small white button
Cockscomb [Celosia argentea cristata]
Columbine [Aquilegia vulgaris]
Cornflower or Bachelors-Button [Centaurea Cyanus]
Crocus
Crown Imperial [Fritillaria imperialis]
Cyclamen
Dames-Rocket [Hesperis matronalis]
Delphinium, [D. elatum], light and dark blue; last half of eighteenth century
Eryngium
Everlasting Pea [Lathyrus latifolius], pink
Forget-me-not
Gentianella [Gentiana acaulis]
Geranium [Pelargonium sp.]
Globe Thistle [Echinops]
Grape Hyacinth
Guelder-Rose or Snowball [Viburnum opulus sterile]
Guinea-hen Flower or Checkered-Lily [Fritillaria meleagris]
Hollyhock, single, double; pink, red, pale yellow
Honeysuckle [Lonicera sp.], Coral
Hyacinth (Dutch or Common), [Hyacinthus orientalis]
Hyacinth (Roman), [Hyacinthus romanus]
Iris, bearded: white florentina, yellow, lavender, blue. Also the Mourning iris [I. susiana]
Iris, bulbous: blue
Jasmine [Jasminum officinale], white
Jasmine [Jasminum sp.], yellow
Johnny-Jump-Up [Viola tricolor]
Larkspur, white, purple
Lilac [Syringa vulgaris], single; lavender, white

Lily-of-the-Valley
Lily [Lilium bulbiferum], upright, orange-red
Lily (Madonna), [Lilium candidum]
Lily (Scarlet Turks-Cap), [Lilium chalcedonicum]
Lily (Turks-cap), [Lilium Martagon]
Love-in-a-Mist [Nigella damascena]
Love-Lies-Bleeding [Amaranthus caudatus]
Maltese Cross [Lychnis chalcedonica], scarlet, white
Marigold (African)
Marigold (French)
Meadow-rue [Thalictrum sp.]
Morning Glory (blue)
Narcissus [N. cyclamineus]
Narcissus [N. incomparabilis], single and double
Narcissus [N. Jonquilla]
Narcissus [N. Pseudo-Narcissus]
Narcissus [N. Tazetta]
Narcissus [N. triandrus]
Nasturtium
Orange
Ox-eye or Field Daisy
Passion Flower [Passiflora]
Peony [Paeonia officinalis] double, single; white, red
Peony [Paeonia albiflora], white, pink; eighteenth century
Periwinkle [Vinca minor]
Pink [Dianthus]
Poppy (Corn Poppy), [Papaver Rhoeas], red, white with red margin
Poppy (opium), [Papaver somniferum]
Ranunculus, yellow, red
Rose, [Rosa alba], semi-double, white
Rose (Cabbage), [Rosa centifolia], double, pink
Rose (Damask), [Rosa damascena], double; white, pink, rose
Rose (Sulphur), [Rosa hemisphaerica], double, yellow
Rose (Apple), [Rosa pomifera], single, pink
Rose-of-Sharon or Shrub Althea [Althea frutex]
Rosemary
Scabiosa
Snowdrop
Snow Flake [Leucojum]
St. Johns Wort [Hypericum]
Stock, single and double, white

Sunflower [Helianthus annuus]
Sweet Sultan [Centaurea moschata]
Teasel
Thistle
Tulip: white, yellow, rose, red; red and yellow Bybloems; rose and white, purple and white Bizarres; occasionally Doubles and Parrots
Trumpet Vine
Tuberose
Veronica
Wild Carrot

FOLIAGE MATERIAL

Aloe
Beech
Cactus
Cyclamen
Grape
Holly
Hollyhock
Hops
Ivy
Peony
Poppy
Ribbon Grass
Rose

FRUITS AND VEGETABLES

Acorns
Artichokes
Asparagus
Blackberries (on branch)
Celery
Cherries
Chestnut (in its bur)
Currants (on branch)
Fig
Gooseberries (on branch)
Gourd (small green-and-white striped)
Grapes (red, blue, green)
Lemon
Maize (corn)
Melon (cut open)
Onions
Orange
Parsnips
Peach
Pineapple
Plum
Pomegranate (often open, to show seeds)
Raspberries (on branch)
Scallions
Strawberries
Walnuts (often with shell open)
Wheat

[1] The best study collection of these flowers is to be found in Ralph Warner's book, *Dutch and Flemish Flower and Fruit Painters of the Seventeenth and Eighteenth Centuries,* London, 1928, Mills and Boon Ltd., and in *The Flower Piece in European Painting* by Margaretta Salinger, New York, 1949, Harper and Brothers.

FRENCH

Seventeenth and Eighteenth Centuries

This list has been compiled from the following volumes: *Le Jardin du Roy Trés Chrestien Henry IV* (Pierre Vallet, 1608); *Livre de Toutes Sortes de Fleurs d'Aprés Nature* (Jean Baptiste Monnoyer, 1660-90); *Le Jardinier Fleuriste et Historiographe, ou La Culture Universelle des Fleurs, Arbres, Arbustes et Arbrisseaux Servans a L'embellissement des Jardins* (Louis Liger, 1748). The author has made a few additions of plant material noted in paintings and engravings.

Anemone [A. coronaria], single, double; white, red
Aster or Michaelmas Daisy [A. Amellus], purple
Auricula or Bears Ears [Primula Auricula], red, purple
Autumn-Crocus [Colchicum]
Balsam [Impatiens Balsamina]
Calendula
Chamomile (Camomile), [Anthemis nobilis]
Canna [C. indica]
Canterbury Bells [Campanula Medium]
Carnation
Cherry, double, white
Christmas-Rose [Helleborus niger]
Chrysanthemum [C. sinense], small white button
Clematis [Clematis sp.]
Cockscomb [Celosia cristata]
Columbine
Cornflower, Bachelors-Button, or Blue-Bottle [Centaurea Cyanus]
Crocus
Crown Imperial [Fritillaria imperialis]
Cyclamen
Dames-Violet or Rocket [Hesperis matronalis]
Datura sp.
Eryngium [E. planum]
Everlasting or Perennial Pea [Lathyrus latifolius], pink
Foxglove
Fraxinella or Gas-Plant [Dictamnus alba]
Gladiolus [G. Byzantinus], dark purple, white
Grape Hyacinth
Guelder-Rose or Snowball [Viburnum opulus sterile]
Guinea-hen Flower or Checkered-Lily [Fritillaria meleagris]
Hollyhock
Honeysuckle [Lonicera sp.], coral

Hyacinth (Dutch), [Hyacinthus orientalis]
Immortelle [Xeranthemum]
Iris, bearded
Iris, bulbous
Jasmine [Jasminum officinale, J. Sambac, J. grandiflorum], white
Larkspur [Delphinium Ajacis], annual, double
Larkspur (Candle or Bee Larkspur), [Delphinium elatum], perennial; dark blue and violet
Lavender
Lilac [Syringa vulgaris], white, lilac
Lily [Lilium bulbiferum]
Lily (Madonna), [Lilium candidum]
Lily (Scarlet Turks-Cap), [Lilium chalcedonicum]
Lily-of-the-Valley
Love-Lies-Bleeding [Amaranthus caudatus]
Maltese Cross or Scarlet Lychnis [L. chalcedonica]
Marguerite [Chrysanthemum frutescens]
Marigold (African), [Tagetes erecta]
Marigold (French), [Tagetes patula]
Marjoram [Origanum]
Marvel-of-Peru or Four-o'Clock [Mirabilis Jalapa]
Monkshood [Aconitum]
Morning Glory
Myrtle [Myrtus communis]
Narcissus [N. incomparabilis], single, double
Narcissus [N. Jonquilla]
Narcissus [N. Pseudo-Narcissus]
Narcissus [N. Tazetta]
Nasturtium
Orange
Passion-Flower [Passiflora]
Pasque-Flower [Anemone Pulsatilla]
Peony [Paeonia officinalis], white, dark red
Peony [Paeonia albiflora], white, pink; eighteenth century

Pheasants-Eye [Adonis]
Pink
Poppy (Red Corn poppy), [Papaver Rhoeas]
Prickly-Poppy [Argemone]
Primrose or Cowslip [Primula veris], red
Princes Feather [Amaranthus hypochondriacus]
Ranunculus
Rose (cabbage), [Rosa centifolia], double, pink
Rose (Rose de Provence), [Rosa centifolia var.] double red
Rose (Chinese Monthly Rose or Bengal Rose), [Rosa chinensis], red to white
Rose (damask), [Rosa damascena], double; white, pink, rose
Rose (Rosa Mundi), [Rosa gallica var. versicolor], white and red striped
Rose (sulphur), [Rosa hemisphaerica], double, yellow
Saffron Crocus [Crocus sativus]
Sage [Salvia officinalis]
Scabiosa
Snapdragon, red, white
Snowdrop
Statice
Stock (white)
Sunflower [Helianthus]
Sweet William
Thyme
Tuberose
Tulip, white, yellow, bi-colors; also parrot
Valerian or Garden-Heliotrope [Valeriana officinalis]
Venus Fly-Trap [Dionaea muscipula]
Violet
Wallflower
Virgins-Bower [Clematis sp.], large-flowered

ENGLISH

Eighteenth Century

Robert Furber's list of flowers grown by him in 1730. Illustrated by Casteels and engraved by Fletcher in *Twelve Months of Flowers*. The names are listed as they appear in the original engravings, with some corrections made in spelling and identification. Words in quotation marks are Furber's original descriptions.

Acacia or Sweet Button Tree [Acacia sp.]
Alaternus [Rhamnus Alaternus argenteo-variegata]

Aloe
Althea frutex or Shrub-Althea (Rose-of-Sharon), [Hibiscus syriacus]

Amaranthus (Josephs-Coat), [A. tricolor]
Anemone [2] [A. coronaria], many varieties

Apios (Groundnut), [A. americana]

Apocinium or Venetian Maritime Dogbane [Apocynum maritimum venetum]

Arbor Judae or Judas-Tree [Cercis sp.]

Arbutus or Strawberry-Tree [Arbutus Unedo]

Arse-smart ("oriental") or Ladys-Thumb [Polygonum Persicaria]

Asphodel or King's Spear [Asphodeline sp.], white, yellow

Auricula [2] [Polyantha Auricula], many varieties

Bachelors-Button [Centaurea Cyanus], blue; or Sweet Sultan [Centaurea moschata], white

Balsam ("double-striped female"), [Impatiens Balsamina]

Bay [Laurus nobilis]

Bluebell Hyacinth (Wood-Hyacinth), [Scilla nonscripta]

Borage

Chamomile (camomile), [Anthemis nobilis], single, double

Canary Bellflower [Campanula canarina]

Canary Shrub Foxglove [Digitalis canariensis]

Candytuft [Iberis sp.]

Cane ("yellow Indian"), [Canna sp.]

Cape Marigold [Dimorphotheca]

Caper ("True, Bean, Bush"), [Capparis sp.]

Cardinal ("Broad-leaved"), [Lobelia cardinalis]

Carnation,[2] many varieties

Carolina Kidney Bean Tree [Robinia sp.], rose-purple

Carolina Starflower (Michaelmas Daisy), [Aster novae-angliae], rose

Catchfly [Silene sp.], double, red

Checquered Fritillary or Guinea-hen Flower [Fritillaria meleagris]

Christmas Flower or Christmas Rose [Helleborus niger]

Christ's Thorn [Paliurus Spina-Christi]

Cinquefoil [Potentilla sp.]

Cockscomb ("yellow amaranthus" and "purple coxcomb amaranth"), [Celosia argentea cristata]

Colchicum, white, yellow; single, double

Colchicum ("striped"), [C. agrippinum majus]

Columbine ("striped"), [Aquilegia vulgaris]

Colutea (Bladder Senna), yellow, scarlet

Convolvulus or Morning Glory, blue, purple

Corn Marigold [Chrysanthemum segetum]

Cornelian-Cherry [Cornus mas]

Cornflower [Centaurea Cyanus], blue

Crocus, white, yellow, blue, striped

Crowfoot ("mountain bulbed"), [Ranunculus asiaticus], double, yellow

Cuccow Flower or Ladies-Smock [Cardamine pratensis]

Cyclamen or Sow Bread, red, white

Cytisus Secundus Clusii (Broom), [Cytisus emeriflorus], yellow

Dogs-tooth Violet [Erythronium dens-canis], red, white

Eternal ("yellow spiked" and "yellow round"), [probably Helichrysum arenarium]

Eternal or Pearly Everlasting [Anaphalis margaritacea]

Feverfew [Chrysanthemum Parthenium]

Fig Marigold or Ficoides [Mesembryanthemum sp.], yellow

Filbert Tree

Flowering Almond [Prunus glandulosa], pink; single, double

Fraxinella, Gas-Plant, or Dittany [Dictamnus], rose

Gentianella [Gentiana acaulis]

Geranium or Cranesbill [Geranium sp.], scarlet, white, purple, black, striped, or "embroidered"

Geranium or Storksbill ("sour-leaved" and "striped-leaved"), [Pelargonium sp.]

Germander [Teucrium]

Glastonbury Thorn [Crataegus monogyna var.]

Globe Amaranth [Gomphrena globosa], red

Globe-Flower [Trollius europaeus], yellow

Golden Knob, unidentified

Grape Hyacinth, blue, white

Greek Valerian [Polemonium caeruleum], white

Groundsel-Tree [Baccharis halimifolia]

Guernsey-Lily [Nerine sarniensis]

Heartsease or Johnny-Jump-Up [Viola tricolor]

Heath ("African"), white, unidentified

Hepatica [H. nobilis], peach, blue, white; single, double

Hollyhock, red, white; single, double

Honeysuckle ("long blowing" and "evergreen"), [Lonicera sp.]

Hop-Hornbeam or American Ironweed [Ostrya virginiana]

Humble-Plant [Mimosa pudica]

Hungarian Climber [Clematis integrifolia]

Hyacinth, (Dutch or Common), [Hyacinthus orientalis], white, blue; single, double

Hyacinth of Peru [Scilla peruviana], white, blue

Indian Tobacco [Nicotiana]

Iris, bearded ("dwarf striped"), [similar to I. variegata], yellow and brown

Iris, bulbous ("velvet Iris, narrow-leaved Flower de Luce, Ultramarine and Prussian blew Iris Major"), [Iris persica var.]

Iris Ulvaria (Poker-Plant or Torch-Lily), [Tritoma or Kniphofia]

Jerusalem Cowslip [Pulmonaria sp.]

Jessamin ("Arabian, Spanish, ivy-leaved"), [Jasminum sp.], white, yellow; single, double

Ketmia [Hibiscus cannabinus], yellow

Larch ("red flowering, white flowering"), [Larix sp.]

Larkspur [Delphinium ajacis], double, blue

Laurestinus [Viburnum Tinus]

Lavender

Lemon Tree ("Lisbon")

Leonorus, Archangel Tree, or Lion's Tail [Leonurus]

Lily [Lilium bulbiferum], double, orange

Lily ("white lily striped with purple"), [Lilium candidum var.]

Lily [Lilium Martagon], reddish purple

Lily (recurved types called "Martagon"), yellow, white, red; single, double

Lily-of-the-Valley, white, blush-red

Lotus [L. tenuis], yellow

Lupine, white

Lychnis ("mountain" and "double scarlet"), [Lychnis sp.]

Maple ("flowering"), American, Virginian, and Norway [Acer sp.]

Marigold (African), yellow

Marigold (French)

Marigold Tree, unidentified

Marvel-of-Peru [Mirabilis jalapa]

Maudlin or Sneezewort [Achillea Ptarmica], double, white

Mezereon [Daphne Mezereum], white, red

Moon Trefoil [Lotus sp.]

Moth Mullein [Verbascum Blattaria]

Mountain Avens [Geum montanum]

Mouse Ear [Primula sp.], double

Myrtle ("Thyme-leaved, Box-leaved"), [Myrtus communis]

Myrto Cistus, unidentified, single, yellow

Naked Boys [Colchicum autumnale]

Narcissus [N. incomparabilis], yellow, bi-color; single, double

Narcissus [N. Jonquilla], yellow; single, double

Narcissus [N. Tazetta], yellow

Nasturtium, single, double

Nigella or Love-in-a-Mist [Nigella damascena]

Oleander, white, red

Olive Tree

Orange Tree ("Seville and striped leaf")

Orchis or Bee Flower [Orchis sp.]

---

[2] The names of anemone, auricula, carnation and tulip varieties may be found in Gordon Dunthorne's *Flower and Fruit Prints of the Eighteenth and Nineteenth Centuries.* Published by the author in Washington, D.C., 1938.

Ox-eye ("Great Spanish"), [Buph-thalmum]
Palma Christi (Castor-Oil-Plant), [Ricinus communis]
Passe-flower [Clematis sp.], white, blue
Passion-Flower [Passiflora]
Peach (double)
Pear
Pellitory [Parietaria], white, yellow
Periwinkle (Running Myrtle), [Vinca sp.], white, blue
Pheasants-Eye [Adonis annua], red
Pilewort [Ranunculus Ficaria]
Pink [Dianthus chinensis and D. plumarius]
Polyanthus (Primrose), [Primula polyantha]
Pomegranate
Poppy [Papaver nudicaule], yellow perennial
Ranunculus, yellow, white, bi-colored, double
Rose ("Blush Belgick" and "Maiden's Blush"), [Rosa alba var.], double, pink
Rose ("Bud Monthly"), [Rosa sp. unidentified]
Rose (Cinnamon), [Rosa cinnamomea], red
Rose ("Double White Musk"), [Rosa moschata]
Rose ("Dutch Hundred leaved"), [Rosa centifolia], red
Rose ("Francford"), [probably Rosa francofurtana], double, red
Rose ("Moss Province"), [Rosa centifolia muscosa]
Rose (Yellow Austrian), [Rosa foetida], single, yellow

Rose (Red Austrian), [Rosa foetida], single, red
Rose (Rosa Mundi), [Rosa gallica versicolor]
Rose ("Striped Monthly" and "White Monthly"), [Rosa chinensis or Rosa bengalensis semperflorens]
Saffron Flower [Crocus sativus]
Sage and Rosemary Tree [Phlomis sp.]
St. Peter's Shrub [probably Symphoricarpos sp.]
Saxifrage [Saxifraga sp.], white
Scabius ("Musk"), [Scabiosa atropurpurea]
Shrub Cotton [Gossypium]
Snowdrop, single, double
Soapwort (Bouncing Bet), [Saponaria officinalis]
Spurge ("striped"), [Pachysandra variegata]
Star-Hyacinth [Scilla amoena], white, blue
Stock, double, red-violet
Strawberry Daisy [probably variety of Bellis perennis]
Sunflower ("Perennial Dwarf"), or Black-eyed Susan, [Rudbeckia hirta]
Sweet Pea, purple
Sweet Sultan [Centaurea moschata]
Sweet William
Throatwort [Trachelium sp.], blue, white; single, double
Tithymal ("Dwarf"), [Euphorbia sp.]
Toadflax [Linaria purpurea]
Tree Primrose [Possibly oenothera sp.], yellow, single
Tree Savory, unidentified
Tree Sedum [Sedum sp.], yellow

Trumpet Flower (Trumpet-Vine), [Campsis radicans]
Tuberose
Tulip[2] (Bybloems, Bizarres, "Dwarf Dutch"), single, double; many varieties
Valerian ("Red, broad-leaved"), [Valerianella sp.]
Vetch ("True Venetian"), [Vicia sp.], red
Viburnum ("American"), [V. trilobum]
Violet, double, blue
Virginian Aster or Michaelmas Daisy [Aster novae-angliae var.], purple
Virginian Birthwort or Snakeroot [Aristolochia sp.]
Virginian Columbine [Not aquilegia], resembles wild carrot
Virginian Flowering Raspberry [Rubus odoratus]
Virginian Poke (Pokeberry), [Phytolacca sp.]
Virginian Scarlet Honeysuckle (Trumpet or Coral Honeysuckle), [Lonicera sempervirens]
Virginian Scarlet Martagon Lily (Tiger Lily), [Lilium tigrinum]
Virginian Shrub Acre, unidentified
Virginian Silk Grass (Spiderwort), [Tradescantia virginiana]
Virginian Stavesacre, unidentified
Virginian Upright Bramble [Rubus occidentalis], single, white
Virgins-Bower (Clematis), [Clematis sp.], single, blue; double, purple
Vitex (Chaste-Tree, [V. Agnus-castus]
Wallflower, single, double
Winter Aconite [Eranthis]
Zisole from Genoa, unidentified

A List of Other Commonly Grown English Flowers Described by John Gerarde, John Parkinson and Philip Miller.

Calendula
Chimney Bellflower [Campanula pyramidalis]
Eryngium
Gladiolus or Common Corn Flag [G. communis], bright purple, flesh
Gladiolus or Corn Flag [G. byzantinus], dark purple
Globe Thistle [Echinops]
Iris [I. florentina], and the Mourning Iris [I. susiana], also blue, purple, and yellow varieties
Larkspur, white, pink, red, purple, blue; single, double
Madonna Lily [Lilium candidum]
Monkshood [Aconitum sp.]
Peach Bells or Peach-leaved Bellflower [Campanula persicifolia]
Peony [Paeonia officinalis], white, red
Snapdragon, white, purple, yellow
Stock, white, yellow, red, purple; single, double

Other Flowers Which Would Have Been Useful as Cut Flowers. Illustrated in the First Ten Issues of Curtis' Botanical Magazine. London 1787-1797.

Alyssum [A. saxatile], yellow
Bee-Balm [Monarda didyma], crimson
Blue Phlox [P. divaricata]
Browallia sp.
Camellia, rose
Chrysanthemum [C. sinense], red-purple
Coreopsis
Great Daffodil [Narcissus Pseudo-Narcissus], yellow
Greater Blue-Bottle [Centaurea montana]
Eastern Poppy [Papaver orientale]
Fuchsia (introduced 1788)
Laburnum or Golden-Chain Tree [L. anagyroides]
Lantana
Lemon Lily or Yellow Day-Lily [Hemerocallis flava]
Lilac [Syringa vulgaris], blue, white, purple
Lupine, yellow, blue
Orange or Tawny Day-Lily [Hemerocallis fulva]
Purple Coneflower [Echinacea sp.]
Statice or Thrift
Virginia Lungwort [Mertensia pulmonarioides]
Zinnia, red, yellow

AMERICAN

Eighteenth Century [3]

Flowers listed in *The Practical Farmer* by John Spurrier, Wilmington, 1793. Dedicated to "Thomas Jefferson, Esq., Secretary of the United States."

Aconite angelica [probably winter aconite, Eranthis]
Agrimony [probably Agrimonia Eupatoria]
Aloe
Amaranthus [species not given; probably Amaranthus caudatus, Love-Lies-Bleeding]
Anemone [A. coronaria]
Asphodel Lily [Asphodelus sp.]
Auricula [Primula Auricula]
Autumn-Crocus [Colchicum autumnale]
Bachelors-Button [Centaurea Cyanus)
Balm of Gilead [probably Melissa officinalis]
Balsam [Impatiens Balsamina]
Basil
Belladonna-Lily [Amaryllis belladonna]
Bottle Gourd
Canterbury Bell [Campanula Medium]
Carnation
China Aster [Callistephus chinensis], white, purple
Christmas-Rose [Helleborus niger]
Chrysanthemum [probably C. sinense]
Columbine
Convolvulus or Morning-Glory
Corona Regalis, unidentified
Crocus

Crown Imperial [Fritillaria imperialis]
Cyclamen
Dogbane or Indian Hemp [Apocynum sp.]
Dogs-tooth Violet [Erythronium dens-canis]
Everlasting Pea [Lathryus latifolius]
French Honeysuckle [Lonicera sempervirens], coral
Gentian
Geranium, no species given
Globe Thistle [Echinops]
Globularia
Goldenrod
Grape Hyacinth
Hollyhock, white, pink, red; single and double
Honesty [Lunaria annua]
Horned-Poppy [Glaucium flavum]
Hyacinth
Iris, bulbous
Lily, no species given
Lily-of-the-Valley
Lupine
Marigold (African), [Tagetes erecta]
Marigold (French), [Tagetes patula]
Mignonette
Milk Vetch or Astragalus [Astragalus sp.]
Molly allium [Allium Moly]
Monkshood [Aconitum]
Narcissus (Jonquil), [N. Jonquilla]
Nasturtium

Nettle-leaved Bellflower [Campanula sp.]
Palma Christi (Castor-Oil-Plant), [Ricinus communis]
Peony [Paeonia officinalis], white, dark red
Pink [Dianthus plumarius]
Polyanthus (Primrose), [Primula polyantha]
Pulsatilla or Pasque-Flower [Anemone Pulsatilla]
Ranunculus
Red-Pepper [Capsicum annuum]
Rocket [Hesperis matronalis]
Rose Campion [Lychnis Coronaria]
Snapdragon
Snowdrop
Solomons-Seal
Squill [probably Scilla sibirica]
Stock
Sweet Scabious [Scabiosa]
Sweet William
Sweet Sultan [Centaurea moschata]
Tree Mallow [possibly Althaea frutex]
Tree Primrose, unidentified
Tuberose
Tulip, double, single, parrot
Valerian or Garden-Heliotrope [Valeriana officinalis]
Veronica
Violet
Wallflower
Zinnia, small yellow, red

The following list has been made up from a number of other sources.

Apple
Azalea (Flame), [Rhododendron calendulaceum]
Azalea (Wild Pink), [Rhododendron nudiflorum]
Bee-Balm or Oswego-Tea [Monarda didyma]
Blue Phlox [Phlox divaricata]
Bouncing Bet [Saponaria officinalis]
Broom
Calendula
Candytuft [Iberis amara], white, annual
Chelone or Turtle-Head, rose-purple
Chaste-Tree (Vitex Agnus-Castus)
Cherry

Clematis or Virgins-Bower [C. virginiana]
Cockscomb [Celosia argentea cristata], crested, plumed
Coreopsis
Crape-Myrtle
Dogwood
English Daisy [Bellis perennis]
Fall Daffodil [Sternbergia lutea]
Foxglove, white, pink, purple
Fraxinella, Gas-Plant, Dittany, or Burning-Bush [Dictamnus]
Globe Amaranth
Guinea-hen Flower or Checkered-Lily [Fritillaria meleagris]
Iris, bearded [blue I. pallida, white I. florentina, purple var.]

Iris, beardless [yellow I. pseudacorus]
Jacobs-Ladder or Greek Valerian [Polemonium caeruleum]
Jasmine (Carolina Yellow Jessamine), [Gelsemium sempervirens]
Jasmine [Jasminum officinale], white
Johnny-Jump-Up
Larkspur
Lemon Lily or Yellow Day-Lily [Hemerocallis flava]
Lilac (Persian), [Syringa persica]
Lilac [Syringa vulgaris], white, lilac, purple
Lily (Madonna), [Lilium candidum]
Lily (Turks-Cap varieties), [Lilium Martagon]

[3] One of the most interesting and complete stories of early American gardening is to be found in Alice G. Lockwood's *Gardens of Colony and State*. Compiled and edited by Mrs. Lockwood for the Garden Club of America, it was published by Charles Scribner's Sons, New York, 1931-34. *Plants of Colonial Days* by Raymond Taylor, and *An Eighteenth Century Garland* by Louise B. Fisher give full information about all the plant materials used at colonial Williamsburg, and much original source material is listed.

Love-in-a-Mist or Devil-in-the-Bush [Nigella damascena]
Magnolia grandiflora
Maltese Cross or Scarlet Lightning [Lychnis chalcedonica]
Marvel-of-Peru or Four o'Clock [Mirabilis Jalapa]
Meadow-Rue [Thalictrum minus]
Mock-Orange [Philadelphus coronarius]
Mountain-Laurel (Kalmia latifolia)
Narcissus [N. incomparabilis], single and double
Narcissus [N. poeticus]
Narcissus [N. Pseudo-Narcissus]
Oleander
Orange
Orange Day-Lily [Hemerocallis fulva]
Pansy or Heartsease

Passion-Flower
Peach
Pear
Peony [Paeonia albiflora], white
Periwinkle or Myrtle [Vinca minor]
Phlox [P. paniculata], pink
Pink Locust
Plum
Poppy [Papaver orientale], orange-red
Primrose [Primula vulgaris]
Quince
Redbud or Judas-Tree
Rose (Dog), [Rosa canina]
Rose (Meadow), [Rosa carolina]
Rose (Cabbage), [Rosa centifolia]
Rose (Eglantine or Sweetbrier), [Rosa Eglanteria]
Rose (Cherokee), [Rosa laevigata]
Rose (Swamp), [Rosa palustris]
Rose (Scotch), [Rosa spinosissima]

Rose-Mallow [Hibiscus Moscheutos]
Rose-of-Sharon or Shrub-Althea [Hibiscus syriacus]
Snowball [Viburnum Opulus sterile]
Southernwood [Artemisia Abrotanum]
Spanish Blueball or Wood Hyacinth [Scilla hispanica]
St. JohnsWort [Hypericum calycinum]
Star-of-Bethlehem (Ornithogalum)
Stewartia
Stokes Aster [Stokesia laevis]
Strawflower
Sweet Pepperbush [Clethra alnifolia]
Sweet-Shrub [Calycanthus floridus]
Sweet Sultan [Centaurea moschata]
Trumpet-Vine [Campsis radicans]
Yarrow
Yucca

First Half of the Nineteenth Century

A list taken from *Flora's Dictionary*, by Elizabeth Washington Wirt, published in Baltimore in 1832. A few additions have been made from *The Flowers Personified*, by Jean Grandville, translated by N. Cleaveland and published in New York City in 1847-1849.

Acacia
African Marigold
Almond
Alyssum saxatile
Amaryllis
Anemone [A. vernalis]
Apple
Auricula [Primula Auricula]
Azalea
Bachelors-Button [Lychnis Dioica]
Balm [Melissa officinalis]
Balsam or Touch-Me-Not [Impatiens Balsamina]
Belvedere or Summer-Cypress [Kochia scoparia]
Blue-Bottle, Cornflower, or Bachelors-Button [Centaurea Cyanus]
Bluets [Houstonia caerulea]
Broom
Buttercup
Calendula
Calla lily
Camellia, red, white
Canterbury Bell, blue, white
Cape-Jasmine [Gardenia florida or G. jasminoides]
Cardinal-Flower [Lobelia cardinalis]
Carnation, rose, deep red
Catalpa
Catchfly [Silene virginica and S. nocturna]
Cherry
China Aster
China-Berry Tree

Christmas Rose [Helleborus]
Chrysanthemum,[4] brown, white, yellow
Clerodendron
Clover, red
Cobaea
Cockscomb
Columbine, purple, red, and yellow
Corchorus [probably Kerria japonica]
Coreopsis
Cowslip [Primula veris]
Cranesbill [Geranium maculatum]
Crape-Myrtle
Crocus
Crown Imperial [Fritillaria imperialis]
Cyclamen
Daffodil (great yellow), [Narcissus Pseudo-Narcissus]
Dahlia
Daisy (common white), [Chrysanthemum Leucanthemum]
Daisy (red), [Bellis perennis]
Dandelion
Daphne odora
Day-Lily or Lemon Lily [Hemerocallis flava]
Dew Plant or Fig-Marigold [Mesembryanthemum]
Dogwood
Evening-Primrose [Oenothera]
Eupatorium
Everlasting [Gnaphalium]

Everlasting Pea [Lathyrus latifolia]
Forget-Me-Not
Foxglove
Fraxinella, Gas-Plant, or Dittany [Dictamnus]
French Marigold
Fringe-Tree [Chionanthus]
Fuchsia
Geranium (Fish), [Pelargonium hortorum]
Geranium (Ivy), [P. peltatum]
Geranium (Nutmeg or Apple), [P. odoratissimum]
Geranium (Oak-leaved), [P. quercifolium]
Geranium (Rose), [P. capitatum]
Geranium (Silver-leaved), [Geranium argenteum]
Gladiolus [5]
Globe Amaranth
Golden-Chain Tree [Laburnum]
Goldenrod
Harebell [probably Campanula rotundifolia]
Hawthorn
Heartsease or Johnny-Jump-Up, yellow, purple, and bi-color
Heliotrope
Hibiscus [H. Trionum]
Hollyhock, red, white
Honesty or Satin-Flower [Lunaria]
Honeysuckle [Lonicera sempervirens], coral

[4] In 1856, *Godey's Lady's Book* mentioned that, since the introduction of chrysanthemums "nearly a hundred years ago," many new sub-varieties had been developed in shades of red, in pure white, yellow and brown. (n.b. there were no pink varieties.) The following seven divisions were noted: (1) Ranunculus-flowered, (2) Incurved, (3) China-Aster-flowered, (4) Marigold-flowered, (5) Clustered, (6) Tapeled, (7) Quilled.

[5] The gladiolus was first exhibited in America in 1834 and was spoken of at the time as a plant with great "promise for the future." By 1863 the following colors were noted in Robert Buist's *Flower Garden Directory:* "yellow, red, scarlet and white, shaded rose, orange, delicate pink, bright scarlet shaded with orange and yellow." Another author mentioned "delicate purple" and "flesh color."

Honey-Flower or Mourning Bride [Melianthus]
Hyacinth, purple, dark blue, rose, white, yellow; feathered
Hydrangea hortensis
Ice-Plant [Mesembryanthemum crystallinum]
Iris,[6] bearded and beardless
Jasmine [Gelsemium], yellow
Jasmine or Poets Jessamine [Jasminum officinale], white
Judas-Tree
Jonquil
Justicia
Lady-Slipper [Cypripedium]
Larkspur, purple, pink
Laurel [Kalmia]
Laurestinus [Viburnum Tinus]
Lavender
Lemon
Lilac [7] [Syringa vulgaris], purple, white
Lilac [Syringa persica]
Lily (Madonna), [Lilium candidum]
Lily (Turban or Turks-Cap), [Lilium Martagon]
Lily-of-the-Valley
Lobelia
Love-in-a-Mist [Nigella]
Love-Lies-Bleeding [Amaranthus caudatus]
Lupine, blue, rose, white
Madagascar Periwinkle [Vinca rosea]
Magnolia grandiflora
Maltese Cross or Scarlet Lightning [Lychnis chalcedonica]
Marsh-Mallow [Althea officinalis]
Marvel-of-Peru or Four o'Clock [Mirabilis Jalapa]
Meadow-Rue [Thalictrum sp.]
Meadow Saffron [Colchicum autumnal]
Michaelmas Daisy [Aster Tradescantii]
Mignonette
Milkweed
Mimosa
Mock-Orange [Philadelphus coronarius]
Monkshood
Morning Glory
Mountain Pink or Cheddar Pink [Dianthus caesius or D. gratiano-politanus]
Mullein
Myrtle
Nasturtium or Indian Cress
Oleander
Orange
Ox-Eye [Buphthalmum]
Passion-Flower
Peach
Pennyroyal [Hedeoma pulegioides or Mentha Pulegium]
Peony,[8] white, pink, red
Periwinkle [Vinca minor], blue, white
Pheasants-Eye or Adonis [Adonis autumnalis]
Phlox [P. paniculata]
Pink [Dianthus chinensis], white, red, variegated
Plumbago
Poets Narcissus [N. poeticus]
Primrose [Primula polyantha], lilac, crimson, rose, yellow
Pomegranate
Poppy (Oriental Poppy), [Papaver orientale]
Poppy (Red Corn Poppy), [Papaver Rhoeas]
Poppy (Opium Poppy), [Papaver somniferum]
Quamoclit or Busybody [Ipomoea coccinea], crimson, white, orange
Queens-Rocket or Dames-Violet [Hesperis matronalis]
Ragged Robin or Cuckoo-Flower [Lychnis Flos-cuculi]
Ranunculus, scarlet
Rhododendron
Rock-Rose [Cistus]
Rose [9] [Rosa alba]
Rose (Cabbage), [Rosa centifolia]
Rose (Moss), [Rosa centifolia muscosa]
Rose (York and Lancaster), [Rosa damascena versicolor]
Rose (Eglantine or Sweetbrier), [Rosa Eglanteria]
Rose (Yellow Sweetbrier), [Rosa foetida or R. lutea]
Rose (Austrian Copper Brier), [Rosa foetida bicolor]
Rose [Rosa inermis Morletti]
Rose (Musk), [Rosa moschata]
Rose [Rosa multiflora]
Rose [Rosa rubrifolia]
Rose Campion or Mullein-Pink [Lychnis Coronaria]
Rose-of-Sharon or Shrub-Althea [Hibiscus syriacus]
Rosemary
Rudbeckia
Sage
Scabious or Mourning Bride, dark purple
Snapdragon, red, white, pink, yellow
Snowball
Snowdrop
Sorrel [Oxalis]
Speedwell [Veronica]
Spiderwort [Tradescantia virginiana]
St. JohnsWort [Hypericum]
Star-of-Bethlehem [Ornithogalum]
Strawberry-Tree [Arbutus Unedo]
Sumac
Sunflower [dwarf, Helianthus Indicus, and tall, Helianthus annuus]
Swamp Magnolia [Magnolia glauca]
Sweet Alyssum
Sweet Pea
Sweet-Shrub or Carolina Allspice [Calycanthus floridus]
Sweet William
Thistle
Thornapple or Jimson-Weed [Datura Stramonium]
Tiger-Flower [Tigridia]
Trollius
Trumpet-Vine [Bignonia radicans and B. crucigera]
Tuberose
Tulip,[10] red, yellow
Tulip-Tree
Venus's Looking-Glass [Campanula Speculum]
Verbena
Violet, blue, white
Virginia Cowslip, American Cowslip, or Shooting-Star [Dodecatheon Meadia]
Virgins-Bower [Clematis virginiana]
Wallflower
Wild Pea (Vetch)
Yarrow
Yucca
Zinnia, yellow, red

---

[6] The nineteenth century produced many new color variations in Iris. Previously, the gray-white of *I. florentina*, the yellow bi-color of *I. variegata* and various purples, blues and lavenders were the only ones known. New varieties included bronzes, maroons, pale yellows, creamy whites, and more bi-colors.

[7] Little lilac hybridization was accomplished before the middle of the nineteenth century. Two old favorites which have never lost their popularity are *Ludwig Spaeth* (deep purple, single) and *Lucie Baltet* (single pink), dating from 1883 and 1888 respectively. The first of the many Lemoine hybrids was originated in 1876.

[8] During the nineteenth century there was much hybridization of peonies. An improved type of the Chinese *Paeonia albiflora* was crossed with the European *Paeonia officinalis* to obtain many new varieties. An early and still well-loved hybrid was the large, double white, *Festiva Maxima* which dates from 1851. The Tree Peony also arrived in America during this century.

[9] In 1848 a New Bedford, Massachusetts, nursery listed the following roses, in addition to those mentioned above: R. arvensis Ayreshirea (Ayrshire), Rosa borboniana (Bourbon), R. chinensis (Chinese Ever-blooming or Bengal), R. gallica (French), R. Noisettiana (Noisette or Champney), R. odorata (Tea).

[10] Bizarres, bybloems, full doubles, and parrots are listed by other authors.

174